This is a Parragon Publishing Book
This edition published in 2001

Parragon Publishing
Queen Street House
4 Queen Street
Bath BA1 1HE, UK

Copyright © Parragon 2000

Created and produced for Parragon by
FOUNDRY DESIGN AND PRODUCTION.

ISBN: 0-75255-144-2

A copy of the CIP data for this book is available from
the British Library, upon request.

The right of Laura Payne to be identified as the author of
this work has been asserted in accordance with Section 77 of the
Copyright, Designs and Patents Act of 1988.

The right of Dr Julia Kelly to be identified as the
author of the introduction to this book has been asserted in
accordance with Section 77 of the Copyright, Designs and
Patents Act of 1988.

Printed and bound in Indonesia.

Essential
CONSTABLE

MANDI GOMEZ

Introduction by Karen Hurrell

P

CONTENTS

INTRODUCTION

JOHN CONSTABLE has been called the father of modern landscape painting; and certainly he is one of the best-known and best-loved English painters, inextricably linked to the modern ideal of the British countryside. But his success was hard won, and he battled against public and critical indifference for most of his career, achieving recognition late in life.

The fourth child of an affluent Suffolk family, he was born on June 11, 1776 in East Bergholt. His childhood was idyllic, and he confessed that in his later years the landscape of his youth evoked "the happy years of the morning of my life". "Constable country', as it is now known, is a 12-mile (19-km) stretch of land around the Stour Valley on the Suffolk–Essex border, and it formed the basis of many of his works. East Bergholt itself was, in Constable's words: "Pleasantly situated in the most cultivated part of Suffolk, on a park which overlooks the fertile valley of the Stour ... The beauty of the surrounding scenery, the gentle declivities, the luxuriant meadow flats sprinkled with flocks and herds ... all impart to this particular spot an amenity and elegance hardly anywhere else to be found".

From an early age, Constable was, to all intents and purposes, an artist. His parents had hopes that he would enter the clergy; when his half-hearted attempts at academia ruled that out, he began training as a miller. His great love remained painting, and his "first youthful wish" was, he said, to become a landscape painter. It is arguable, however, that he had little natural talent. His first efforts at defining his environment on paper were uninspired. Despite the limits of his draftsmanship, however Constable had vision. He took an academic approach to his work, and, fostered by close friendships with men who shared his dream, he nurtured an interest that became a passion and then a very real talent. As a youth, his closest friend was John Dunthorne, the local plumber, with whom he shared an enthusiasm for outdoor study. They worked hard together, taking their easels with them into the fields and painting one view only for a certain time each day. David Lucas (1802–81), Constable's engraver, noted that: "When the shadows from objects changed, their sketching was postponed until the same hour next day."

Like Claude Monet (1840–1926) and the Impressionists, Constable believed that landscapes must be painted *en plein air*, that is, painted in natural light, out-of-doors. At the time, English landscape painters produced idealized studies of nature, based on study rather than first-hand experience. Indeed, Constable himself claimed that his early work consisted of "running after pictures and seeking the truth second hand". Claude Lorrain (1600–82) was a great influence on the English landscape artists, as was the 17th-century Dutch painter Jacob van Ruisdael (*c.* 1628–82), and there were accepted conventions about how every aspect of nature should be painted and composition organized. Here, Constable's limitations became strengths. His poor draftsmanship meant that he painted what he saw rather than what he thought he should paint. He believed in imbuing his art with a passionate symbolism that brought a painting to life. Constable's paintings had a directness and integrity that would surely have been absent had he learned his craft from a young age, or had a natural affinity with the art of his contemporaries.

In the early 19th century, landscape painting was neither lucrative nor regarded highly. It is a measure of his commitment and achievement that Constable's painting finally became acceptable, but during his lifetime it was a source of great personal dissatisfaction that he was unable to earn a living by his craft. As a young adult, Constable, like many of his peers, attended the Royal Academy Schools, where he was taught to draw correctly from prints, plaster casts and life models. Through dedicated practice he learned the art of form and in 1800 wrote: "I find it necessary to fag at copying, some time yet, to acquire execution."

He was an avid student, reading Salomon Gessner's *Essay on Landscape* (1798), and following its advice when copying from landscape engravings. He befriended Sir George Beaumont, one of his earliest patrons, who was a great influence. An amateur artist whose work appeared regularly at the Royal Academy, he offered practical advice and sound artistic direction to his protogé. Joseph Farington (1747–1821), a mutual friend, saw his influence in Constable's work, writing that Constable's trees were, "so like Sir George Beaumont's that they might have been taken for his". He absorbed the best of the landscape art that preceded him, but imbued it with his own integrity. Thomas Gainsborough (1727–88) was a favorite, and much of Constable's early work, including *A Wood* (1802), shows his influence.

When Constable decided to concentrate on observed nature, he  was forced to invent a new manner of working that permitted him to express the transient effects of light and shade on the landscape. The specks and strokes of white paint that lie on the surface of his landscapes were one of the means by which he tried to capture the freshness that fascinated him.

Constable earned very little from his art, relying on allowances from his family. Later in his life, he sought the hand of Maria Bicknell, who came from a good Suffolk family who made it clear that Constable would need to earn a good living for her to consider his marriage proposals. Their courtship ended in marriage only when the deaths of family members allowed them an inheritance upon which to live. He supplemented his father's allowance by producing drawings that were sold to the public by a local firm, and over a 15-year period undertook a series of portrait commissions, which he regarded as an unfortunate necessity.

In 1801, Constable toured the Derbyshire Peak District, producing light and airy sketches which are now regarded as immature work. The following year marked the foundation of the values that eventually defined his style. He wrote to Dunthorne in May of that year: "I shall return to Bergholt, where I shall endeavor to get a pure and unaffected manner of representing the scenes that may employ me. There is room

enough for a natural *peinture*". His convictions strengthened, and he began to paint direct studies from nature with the aim of putting down exactly what he saw. He had no preconceived ideas about how a picture should look and he kept a fidelity to nature as he saw it. His paintings lack the composition of his contemporaries, but they retain a freshness that is true to life.

In 1806, Constable visited the Lake District, and despite the fact that he felt "oppressed" by the mountains and spectacular scenery of the lakes, he produced some of his most significant work to date. The grandeur of the Lake District has inspired countless centuries of artists. Constable concentrated on studying the weather and the atmosphere of the mountains, noting the atmospheric conditions on the back of his paintings—a habit he continued for the rest of his life. His paintings were rough, spontaneous, and painted quickly, as the weather shifted.

Between 1810 and 1815 Constable spent most of his summers at East Bergholt, sketching in the fields and the countryside. This period was marked by his need to paint without preconception. He showed a lack of interest in the effects of light, tone, and color, concentrating instead on his impression and experience of nature as a basis for his work. Earlier paintings were disappointingly flaccid, with weak, pale skies as a backdrop. Constable's new work concentrated on creating skies that were an integral part of the work. He painted and sketched many studies of clouds and skies in all shades and hues. He departed from the traditions of painting by discarding the usual brown underpainting and achieving natural, luminous lighting effects through the use of broken color applied with a palette knife. He endeavored

to portray the effect of the scene, often softening physical details. He was fascinated by reflections in water and light on clouds, and his greatest works undoubtedly inspired the Impressionists.

Constable's sketches were the basis for his compositions, and he extensively used the "oil sketch" for his most enduring and satisfying works. *Boat-Building Near Flatford* (1815) marked an attempt to produce a finished picture in the open air, giving his subject the immediacy of a sketch but with the detail and lustre of a well-thought-out study. It is one of his less successful paintings, probably because it works best as a series of details rather than a comprehensive whole, but it indicated the breadth of his vision and dedication to producing art that was direct and spontaneous. His oil sketches were not produced to define his composition; rather, they produced a soft, brown base on which to work; an attempt to capture the directness and freshness of the moment.

In 1816, Constable finally married Maria Bicknell, and found a deep satisfaction that had been missing in his life. Although he was short-tempered, idealistic, and inflexible when it came to his art, he found solace in the combination of family and work. In 1823 he wrote: "I have a kingdom of my own both fertile and populous—my landscape

and my children". Following his marriage, he turned away from
realistic agrarian landscapes such as *Ploughing Scene* (1814), due in part
to the fact that more and more of his time was spent in London, and in
part to the depression and riots that affected landowners and farmers
across the country, changing the nature of his agrarian ideal.

On the advice of friends, he made a decision to increase the size
of his paintings. He was aware that his election to the Academy was long
overdue, and the disinterest in his paintings by his contemporaries left
him embittered. He sought a means by which to draw attention to the
detail of his work by producing ambitious paintings of a size normally
designated for "historical" landscapes or other "worthy" subjects.

His first large painting was *Flatford Mill* (1816–17), and it captured
the interest of critics and fellow artists. Although the painting did not
sell, Constable realised that large-scale, grandiose canvases might just be
sufficient to make the art world take note. *The White Horse* (1817) was
his first 6-ft (1.8-metre) painting, and it was exhibited in 1819 to the
first positive critical attention the artist had received. *The White Horse*
compelled the Royal Academy to take Constable's approach seriously,
and he was finally elected an Associate in 1819. Shortly afterwards, he
received a large sum from his father's estate, and his new prosperity
allowed him to rent Albion Cottage in Hampstead.

Stratford Mill was the second of Constable's large canvases, shown
at the Academy in 1820. Avoiding the rural scenes of well-tilled fields
and farm laborers, he chose instead
young anglers as his subject. In
1821, he exhibited *The Haywain*
under the title *Landscape: Noon*. It
evolved from a full-size sketch to
a rich, compelling painting that
was both grand and vigorous.
Some critics claimed that the
work lacked "finish', but from this
time on, Constable produced full-
size studies in preparation for his

final exhibited work. *The Haywain* is the best-known of Constable's paintings and became a statement of his personal vision. He attained the freshness of a landscape under changing skies with his usual complete fidelity to nature.

If the English establishment failed to understand his approach, while grudgingly admitting its appeal, the Europeans were enchanted. In 1822, the painting was purchased by the French art dealer John Arrowsmith, who exhibited it at the Paris Salon in 1824. It won the gold medal and was admired by such artists as Eugène Delacroix (1798–1863) and Théodore Géricault (1791–1824). The rising generation of French Romantic painters was impressed by his handling of paint and rendering of light and shade in bright colors. Delacroix repainted parts of his *Scenes from the Massacre at Chios* (1824) after seeing the Constable paintings. He became a force in the regeneration of French landscape painting effected by the Barbizon school.

From here, Constable moved away from his exact rendering of nature as he saw it. In 1825, he exhibited *The Leaping Horse* (1825), and a comparison between the sketch and the final painting shows that he moved trees and barges to make the composition more pleasing, and to provide a depth that was lacking in the original. But if he was forced by the sheer size of his canvases to do more work in the studio, away from his beloved nature, he retained the ability to impose a passion upon his paintings. His subject-matter never really changed, and he continued to find beauty in all that surrounded him. In an 1836 lecture, he stated: "It was said by Sir Thomas Lawrence that "we can never hope to compete with nature in the beauty and delicacy of her separate forms or colors—our only chance lies in selection and combination." Nothing can be

more true ... I have endeavored to draw a line between genuine art and mannerism, but even the greatest painters have never been wholly untainted by manner. Painting is a science, and should be pursued as an inquiry into the laws of nature."

He became passionate about landscapes outside the Stour Valley as he traveled—Weymouth and the nearby village of Osmington were places where he spent time with his family, and was never without his sketch-pad and oils. Salisbury, the later home of his friend John Fisher, was another favorite subject, as was Brighton, where his wife stayed after 1824 as her health began to decline. Hampstead Heath, his London home of the 1820s, inspired some of his most exciting studies and paintings. He never traveled abroad, and found everything he required in the counties that surrounded his home.

In 1828, Maria died of tuberculosis following the birth of their seventh child, and Constable was plunged in to overwhelming sorrow. The following year he exhibited *Hadleigh Castle* (1829), a stormy painting that reflected his gloom. The same year he was belatedly elected a Royal Academician, and although he took his professional responsibilities seriously, he remained detached from the Academy, finding it difficult to forget the disappointment of being awarded full membership so late. He wrote: "It has been long delayed, until I am solitary and cannot impart it."

In many of his later paintings, Constable returned to earlier sketches. His *Stonehenge* (1836) derives from a sketch made in 1820, and *Cenotaph* of 1836, a tribute to Joshua Reynolds (1723–92), is based on a drawing made at the country home of Sir George Beaumont in 1823. It may be that Constable was trying to reclaim some of the inspiration of his earlier years, deadened to some extent by the death of his wife, and shortly afterwards, by that of John Fisher. But he also felt an urge to experiment with light, shade and color, becoming, in his later years, more mannerist in his attempts to be original. In the last years of his life, he became obsessed with demonstrating his versatility and the potential of his genre. He issued an unsuccessful series of engravings with accompanying text in which he emphasised the importance of the "*chiaroscuro* in nature."

For Constable, *chiaroscuro* (the treatment of light and shade) was an effect to be obtained at all costs; in the pursuit of this, he evolved an expressive execution, including the impastoed flecks of white which offended his contemporaries. This was particularly true of his work after the 1820s, when his subjects moved away from the logic of external reality. Delacroix commented that: "Constable says that the superiority of the greens in his meadows is due to the fact that they are made up of a large number of different greens. What gives a lack of intensity and life to the verdure of the ordinary run of landscape painters is that they do it with a uniform tint." This is, surely, one of Constable's major technical achievements and a style of painting that would, eventually, make the English landscape a genre in its own right.

Constable's landscape had always been sentimental and personal. His later work, however, took on a more historical association, opening up his paintings to a public sympathy and experience. These works are much closer in nature to those of J. M. W. Turner (1775–1851) and Joshua Reynolds, both of whom used allusions to create an elevated landscape. He became interested in broad masses of light and shade, and his attention to detail declined. *A River Scene, with a Farmhouse Near the Water's Edge* (c. 1835) illustrates his use of broken color, thick paint and expressionistic handling. He became melancholic about his abilities to transform the vision of nature into a painting, and in 1831 he wrote: "Nothing can exceed the beauty of the

country—it makes pictures seem sad trumpery." When his paintings failed to be as true to nature as he wished, he felt a sense of failure, and his distrust for sophisticated images left him frustrated. *Hadleigh Castle* (1829) marked the beginning and also ther end of his romantic expressionism, and was, to some extent, his last great masterpiece. Later works are rich with meaning, but missing his heart-felt passion. Constable was preparing a view of *Arundel Mill and Castle* when he died on March 31, 1837. Although he had suffered ill-health for many years, in particular crippling rheumatism, his death was still unexpected and is believed to have been caused by a sudden heart attack.

He had a taste of fame in the last years of his life, and wrote with some degree of prophecy in 1829: "The rise of an artist in a sphere of his own must almost certainly be delayed; it is to time generally that the justness of his claims to a lasting reputation will be left; so few appreciate any deviation from the beaten track." He was the first major English artist to concentrate on rural scenes without using historical associations, and was also the first artist to paint such scenes on the scale usually reserved for recording important events in history. He established a highly individual technique and approach to portraying nature, and, although never fully appreciated in his lifetime, his method has become legendary, and his paintings proof that English domestic scenery is a legitimate vehicle for serious ideas and ideals.

KAREN HURRELL

DANIEL GARDNER
Portrait of John Constable, R. A.,
Aged Twenty (1796)
Courtesy of the V & A Picture Library/Mr D. P. P. Naish

DANIEL Gardner was a student at the Royal Academy and later a Royal Academician. He was senior to Constable by about 15 years. Constable was friendly with his son, George Gardner, with whom he visited the Lake District in 1806. This small portrait remained in Constable's possession until after his death, when it was given to the Victorian and Albert Museum by his daughter Isobel.

Daniel Gardner was an established portrait painter and his small portraits in oil or crayon were very fashionable at the time. This was probably painted for Constable as a keepsake from his friend and colleague. Gardner depicts a youthful and intelligent young man against a dark background, sitting slightly oblique to the picture plane. He was well-known for such elegant compositions as the one employed here showing a relaxed, informal, and youthful Constable. His facial features are delicately drawn and his youth and vigor are suggested by the pink-yellow palette against a dark background.

This portrait, when considered with what is probably a self-portrait, *Portrait of the Artist Half-length in a Black Coat* (C. 1806–09) throws up some interesting similarities and changes in the artist's appearance. The nose is similar in both paintings. In the Gardner portrait, the artist has more hair and his face is fuller and more youthful. Here, we know that Constable is aged 20 years old, which helps us to surmise that the later self-portrait was drawn somewhere around 1816–20 when he was in his late thirties or early forties.

The Valley of the Stour, Looking Towards East Bergholt (1800)
Courtesy of the V & A Picture Library

THIS pen and watercolor drawing and the one that follows were made by Constable as a wedding present for a friend, Lucy Hurlock, who, like himself, grew up in Suffolk. There are four drawings that make a complete panorama of the Stour Valley from west to east, stretching from Langham church to the estuary. Each drawing contains a single view; this one looks east, with East Bergholt church and Old Hall visible in the background.

A path in the foreground leads the eye through a small gap between a fence and a bushy hedge to a private garden. There are some cows grazing. If we follow this path, the vista opens out into a flat landscape through the trees and fields past more grazing sheep and cattle and on towards East Bergholt church.

The watercolor is gently laid on to the canvas to highlight aspects of the pen drawing. Some paper is visible and the watercolor wash has been used with sensibility. Color is used to accent certain parts of the drawing: the yellow roof of the house on the right, the clump of green grass under the tree on the left, the delicate green in the mid-ground, lit by the moving clouds. There is a sense of movement in the sky, washed very delicately in white-blue and gray, which skits across the landscape altering the light and color of the familiar Suffolk landscape.

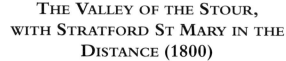

THE VALLEY OF THE STOUR, WITH STRATFORD ST MARY IN THE DISTANCE (1800)

Courtesy of the V & A Picture Library

THIS is the second pen and watercolor drawing belonging to a series of four that present a complete panorama of the Stour Valley from west to east. Constable gave them to his friend, Lucy Hurlock, on the occasion of her marriage in November 1800. To mark this day, Constable wanted to give Lucy a present that would give her an accurate survey of the landscape where she grew up. Always sentimental about the landscape in Suffolk, he presented her with drawings that are both topographically accurate and exquisitely drawn.

The series takes much from the techniques of the 17th-century Dutch landscape artist, Jacob van Ruisdael (1628/29–82) and, in that the viewpoint is low, the foreground is in microscopic detail, while also showing the immensity of the landscape in the general composition. Constable, like Van Ruisdael, believed that man was insignificant beside the majesty and power of nature, hence the trees, hills and dales, rivers, and ponds have greater significance than humankind.

The foreground bush and scrub opens into a view identified as the coach road to Stratford St Mary at the point where it crosses the Stour, with the village church on the right.

ACADEMY STUDY OF A NUDE MALE FIGURE (C. 1800)

Courtesy of the V & A Picture Library

$\mathcal{I}$N 1799 Constable's father finally consented to his devoting himself fully to the study of art. His career as a painter began with his independent copying of works by Raphael (1483–1520) and Claude Lorrain (1600–82), which was an essential part of Academy training. He also attended anatomy classes in London and, of course, the obligatory life-study classes, which resulted in this nude study.

There are some amusing anecdotes relating to the keepers (or tutors) at the Academy schools. One in particular relates to the dynamic and somewhat eccentric Henry Fuseli (1741–1825), who would not tolerate what he called "a neegeling tooch" or undefined outline in his pupils' work.

In this study, Constable's outline is somewhat "neegeling", although his use of light and shade is confident and appropriate. His discomfort with drawing the human form can be seen, and it is evident throughout his career that he is not happy with portraiture. The figures that appear often in his landscape compositions are part of, if not subsidiary, to the role of nature. This study is somewhat stiff and awkward. The model's foot, propped up on a block, is wooden.

Academy Study of a Nude Male Figure (c. 1800)
Courtesy of the V & A Picture Library.
(See p. 24)

ACADEMY STUDY OF A NUDE MALE FIGURE (C. 1800)
Courtesy of the V & A Picture Library

*T*HIS study of a male figure with his head resting in his hand is drawn in black and white chalk on brown paper. The medium provided Constable with the means to highlight and shade dramatically. The use of *chiaroscuro*, or treatment of light and shade, is an essential part of Constable's work; for any drawing or composition to be without the effects of light and shade appears to have been incomprehensible to him.

The posture of the sitter is translated eloquently by Constable's use of the chalks and paper, which seem to allow him to work more naturally and with greater ease than the preceding study in charcoal. The shadow of the figure's lower body is well-positioned against the blocks, accentuating the diagonal of the outstretched arm and ratio of the bent arm's elbow to the knee of the outstretched leg. Similarly, the diagonal between the bent knee and the outstretched arm is well placed.

The outlines for this study are confidently drawn, which may be why it was originally dated with later work of around 1820, but it is now placed with the Academy studies of the early 1800s. Later in his career Constable undertook portraits, like *The Baker Children* (date unknown) to bolster his rather precarious finances but was never really happy painting the human torso.

***The Barker Children* (Date Unknown)**
Courtesy of Christie's Images. (See p. 41).

THE VALLEY OF THE STOUR, WITH DEDHAM IN THE DISTANCE (C. 1800–1805)

Courtesy of the V & A Picture Library

THIS rather "toy-townish" view of the Stour Valley probably predates the letter quoted with *The Wood* (*c.* 1802). This refers to Constable's intention to follow his own artistic sensibilities and it illustrates his resolve to not bow to his critics or to make his work appear "made by other men" simply in order to gain respect and admiration. This is an important departure from what may be viewed in the present sketch as wooden, self-conscious painting.

The view, tentative in its drawing but pleasing compositionally, looks towards Dedham, with Stratford St Mary bridge dividing Suffolk from Essex in the foreground. The red-brown bank and trees in the foreground are evidently suffering from age. The device of the built-up bushes or trees on the right limits our view clumsily and acts as a boundary rather than an invitation into the painting.

The river meanders as far as the eye can see diagonally across the canvas. The trees, unstructured and without Constable's familiar eye for detail, become illustrative rather than emotive. The palette is light and bright, but almost too much so, the water of the river is unreasonably blue and does not reflect the pinkish sky, the greens are over-bright and the brick-red of the buildings garish.

DEDHAM VALE (1802)
Courtesy of the V & A Picture Library

*U*NUSUALLY for Constable, this landscape showing Dedham Vale is painted portrait, rather than landscape, and the dimensions work very well for this composition, which is derived from Claude's *Landscape with Hagar and the Angel*. Apparently, at this time, Constable was copying fellow artist and patron Sir George Beaumont's (1753–1827) "small upright Claude', now in the National Gallery, London.

Both this painting and *Dedham Vale: Evening* (1802) are studies, not sketches, and they convey Constable's commitment to the study of the great masters, Jacob van Ruisdael and Claude, in particular. However, Constable was a protégé of Sir Joshua Reynolds (1723–92), who insisted upon an artist's responsibility to resist following the masters of the past slavishly, but to surpass them by studying nature. Constable took to heart Reynolds' teachings and considered that: " ... nature had been 'the fountainhead from whence all our ideas are derived'."

Painted from a high viewpoint, Dedham Vale meanders across the

canvas with the line of the river: a wavy, lingering line which takes the eye on a journey through the picture, guiding us through the landscape to Dedham church in the distance. The trees and foliage that frame the scene are bathed in soft September light.

Dedham Vale: Evening (1802)
Courtesy of the V & A Picture Library. (See p. 30)

DEDHAM VALE: EVENING (1802)
Courtesy of the V & A Picture Library

*T*HE landscapes of 1802 are very important in Constable's career as a professional landscape artist. The *Discourses* of Sir Joshua Reynolds and William Hogarth's (1697–1764) *Analysis of Beauty,* published in 1753, influenced Constable's career in that he took personal responsibility for making English landscape painting a revered and respected artistic genre. Although these influences are critical, Constable's commitment to painting in the open air from nature to communicate the "truth" in what he saw—the light that bathed the scene and the sense of the place itself—were to mark his work for the entirety of his career. To convey this "truth" was for Constable the very crux of what being an artist was all about.

Just before his arrival in Bergholt to paint this and the companion landscape *Dedham Vale* (1802), Constable wrote that he would: "Shortly return to Bergholt where I shall make some laborious studies from nature—and I shall endeavor to get a pure and unaffected representation of the scenes that may employ me ..." It is this purity that Constable wishes to convey.

Dedham Vale: Evening was painted during an evening in July. There are shafts of sunlight landing on the undulating fields; the early evening light is gentle and there are no harsh lines or colors.

A MILL ON THE BANKS OF THE RIVER STOUR (1802)

Courtesy of the V & A Picture Library

*T*HIS black chalk and charcoal drawing of 1802 was drawn at noon on October 3rd and was probably finished away from the location. It is possible that Constable made an oil painting from this drawing which is now lost. An engraving of the subject, similarly composed, was published in 1810.

The drawing is in the style of an untrained, but popular, contemporary artist and friend of Constable's, George Frost (1743–1821), whom Constable admired greatly, and several of whose pictures he owned. Their styles were said to be very similar, which is noticeable in this drawing.

The drawing uses the white paper and black chalk to express the lights and darks of the scene. The windmill on the bank is reflected in the water, which is still and bright, contrasting with and reflecting the sky.

In the foreground are some posts, which appear to be standing on the bank. The bank then swings around to the left, rising as it does so on to the higher ground of the mill. A tree stump or post encloses the left-hand side of the composition.

VALLEY SCENE, WITH TREES (1802)
Courtesy of the V & A Picture Library

*T*HIS valley is probably near Dedham, and was painted in the open air during Constable's visit in the autumn of 1802. The painting is generally regarded as being the outcome of Constable's resolve to follow his own artistic and philosophical beliefs: "For these past two years I have been running after pictures and seeking the truth at secondhand. I have ... endeavored to make my performances look as if really executed by other men ...."

The composition shows the influence of Claude in its use of the trees to create the frame within which the valley can flourish as a picture. Some shepherds or other motifs of Arcadia would not appear out of place in this landscape. Constable, however, is trying to relay to us here the "truth" of the scene, not reinventing a past age or style.

In comparison with later landscapes, such as *Taylor Ghyll, Sty Head, Borrowdale* (1806), the color is deep and lustrous; the Lake District sketches were executed in pencil and gray and pink wash.

The brown ground of the painting shows through the wondrously built-up greens of the landscape. The colors are autumnal and rich, and include yellow, brown, orange, and several shades of green. The sky is blue and white with a hint of pale blue-mauve, which is repeated on the horizon.

Taylor Ghyll, Sty Head, Borrowdale (1806)
Courtesy of the V & A Picture Library. *(See p. 42)*

A WOOD (C. 1802)

Courtesy of the V & A Picture Library

*T*HIS beautifully composed early sketch by Constable of a wood, probably near Dedham, in the early morning, was possibly painted in September 1802. The painting shows his firm resolve to follow his own artistic path. He concentrated on making studies straight from nature and capturing the colors accurately.

The rough canvas shows through the paint, giving the foreground a deep brown-red color suggestive of fallen leaves and layer upon layer of rotting vegetation on the ground. The trees are leafy and their density allows no view beyond the wood. The eye travels upwards along the trees instead of towards the blue, slightly cloudy sky.

The palette comprises a plethora of greens in the mid-ground, with the leaves of the trees highlighted in a soft yellow. The foreground colors reveal pink, some off-white, dark green and black, which delineates the pathway leading left to right through the composition. The sky, a beautiful soft blue with white and pale blue-gray cloud, contrasts beautifully with the green of the trees. Likewise, the green is in harmonious contrast to the red foreground.

SUSANNAH LLOYD (1806)

Courtesy of the Tate Gallery, London

*T*HIS serene portrait of Susannah Lloyd marks the beginning of Constable's career as a professional painter. The sitter is the daughter-in-law of the Birmingham banker, Charles Lloyd Senior. Constable met his son, Charles Junior through the Hardens of Brathay Hall in the Lake District, where he stayed during the tour financed by his maternal uncle, David Pike Watts.

Constable was to rely on an income from portraiture for some years to come, but his inability to capture the sitter's facial features in this painting is obvious. The posture and clothing are competent, however, and show the influence of Sir Joshua Reynolds, to whom Constable would look with an eye to his painting technique and also to his *Discourses*, his published lectures from the Royal Academy, where Reynolds was the first president.

During 1807, Constable was commissioned by the Dysart family to copy portraits by Reynolds and John Hoppner (1758–1810), and his study of Reynolds became ever more apparent in his work. Constable also took Reynold's advice on the true rendering of a landscape.

Head of a Girl (c. 1806–09)
Courtesy of the V & A Picture Library
(See p. 48)

THE BARKER CHILDREN (DATE UNKNOWN)
Courtesy of Christie's Images

*T*HIS portrait of around 1805 may be a product of Constable's continued efforts to meet his family's wishes to establish himself as a portrait-painter. Portrait painting was the only sure way of making a living as a painter at the time, and Constable may have agreed to this commission for no other reason than to earn the fee. The patron, it is supposed, was sufficiently well off to employ Constable to paint this portrait of his children to mark a special event. Sophia, the eldest, appears to be the subject of this painting and it may be that she is "coming-out" and that this painting is in celebration of the occasion. Constable's attention to established English portrait painters such as Joshua Reynolds and Thomas Gainsborough (1727–88) is evident in the treatment of costume and facial features.

The children are well grouped, with Sophia on the left gently touching her younger brother's shoulder. She has a maternal and protective air, and the authority of an elder sister who has been given an adult role to play. The young boy, Benjamin, teeters on the sofa in his little red shoes, supported and protected by his two sisters. The top of his white suit falls off his shoulders, revealing his plump upper chest. His chubby arms are awkwardly painted although their general positioning and stance are plausible.

Harriet, not yet a teenager, is somewhat marginalised on the right of the composition. Her short hair and the high-necked shirt under a black smock are conventional contemporary attire for young girls and she lacks the elegance of her elder sister, with her fashionable coiffeur and full-length black dress.

TAYLOR GHYLL, STY HEAD, BORROWDALE (1806)

Courtesy of the V & A Picture Library

*D*URING 1806 Constable had a busy summer visiting friends and family in East Bergholt in June, Tottenham in July and Epsom in August. By September he was in the Lake District spending time at Lake Windermere and continuing on to Borrowdale with George, the son of the portrait painter, Daniel Gardner, who painted *Portrait of Constable, R. A., Aged Twenty* (1796).

This view depicts Borrowdale in Cumbria, a place surrounded by hills in a deep valley. Here, Constable had incredible scenery and dramatic weather conditions to paint; both elements evidently inspired him. These drawings are very beautiful.

View in Borrowdale (1806)
Courtesy of the V & A Picture Library. (See p. 44)

(See p. 44)

This sketch is in pencil and gray and pink wash, and pays homage to Thomas Girtin (1775–1802), who had a revolutionary influence on English landscape painting in watercolor.

In 1902, critic Sir Charles Holmes made a statement about the importance of the mountainscape drawings made by Constable during this period: " It is hard to think of any other drawings in which the peculiar characteristics of English mountain scenery have been more grandly expressed. Such scenery is ... exceedingly difficult to paint ... Constable overcame this difficulty with wonderful skill, utilizing for his purpose all the devices which lowering clouds, drifting mists, sudden bursts of light, broad spaces of mysterious shadow, and the flash of water far away provide for the impressionable mind."

VIEW IN BORROWDALE (1806)

Courtesy of the V & A Picture Library

CONSTABLE visited Cumberland specifically to draw—the tour was financed by his uncle, David Pike Watts. The stay lasted seven weeks, during which time he produced about 90 known works. Constable arrived at Borrowdale at the end of his stay in the Lakes, with his friend, George Gardner, son of the portrait-painter Daniel Gardner, who after a few days "got tired of looking on" and left Constable to get on with his work alone.

The sketches executed during this visit are remarkable. To paint the weather, how it effected the light and therefore the colors of the landscape were Constable's *raison d'être* as a painter throughout his

career. This long, panoramic watercolor and pencil sketch captures the hills of Cumbria just as the rain has stopped. The cloud breaking throws winter light on to the craggy hills, and the air seems to be sodden and heavy. The landscape peels open from the center, the massive hills descend, opening in the center, and rise on the left and right edges of the picture.

The palette of green, brown, and gray used against the white background of the paper in this painting creates a mellow harmony of tone that dramatizes the stunning enormity of the landscape and captures the transient effect of the clouds.

HIS MAJESTY'S SHIP *VICTORY* (1806)
Courtesy of the V & A Picture Library

*T*HIS watercolor, exhibited at the Royal Academy in 1806, is Constable's closest approximation to formal painting after battles or historical events. In contrast, water-colorist J. M. W. Turner (1775–1851), Constable's contemporary, turned such great events like his *Snowstorm: Hannibal and His Army Crossing the Alps* (exhibited at the Royal Academy in 1812) into philosophical and political statements.

Constable was a realist. He did not want his view of the Battle of Trafalgar to portray anything but the battle. Constable's brother Abram reckoned that the idea "was suggested to him by hearing an account of the battle from a Suffolk man who had been in Nelson's ship."

The picture shows the point when the battle is raging. The ships begin to line up; there is a moment of tension implicit in the composition, the smoky, gray atmosphere and the dilapidated-looking ships about to enter battle. The ships are painted in a fair amount of detail, with their rigging rising up to the sky compositionally and creating a triangle in the gray-yellow sky, with *Victory* at its pinnacle at the center of the picture.

HEAD OF A GIRL (C. 1806–09)

Courtesy of the V & A Picture Library

*T*HIS portrait of a young woman is probably Constable's younger sister, Mary. The approximate date of the picture, *c.* 1806–09, is based on the girl's coiffeur, which is in a style fashionable at this time. Likewise her costume; the puffed short sleeve of her dress can just be seen and is in keeping with the fashions of around 1806.

Mary Constable, probably sitting with her back to the artist, turns her head slightly; her profile is sweetly caught as if she is glancing behind at the viewer. The rendering of the shape of her face is a little uncomfortable, but the portrait manages to portray the sitter's youth and charm. The flesh tones are plausible, but her hair is clumsily highlighted and the background interferes with the shape of her head. The sitter's eyes are shiny, intelligent, and bright, her skin delicate and soft, and her hairstyle fashionable and tidy. Her general demeanor is one of a middle-class girl with youth and integrity, much like a character from a Jane Austen novel.

At the time the portrait was painted, Constable was copying portraits by Joshua Reynolds and John Hoppner of the Dysart family. The techniques learned from these two established English portrait painters almost certainly influenced this portrait.

PORTRAIT OF THE ARTIST HALF-LENGTH
IN A BLACK COAT (C. 1806-09)
Courtesy of Christie's Images

IT IS not absolutely certain that this portrait is of Constable, or that it is actually by him. There is a drawing of 1806, which is certainly a self-portrait, accomplished through a complicated device of mirrors in order for the artist to portray himself. This painted portrait appears to be unfinished and does not bear a signature or date to authenticate it absolutely.

Further known portraits of Constable exist, one by John Harden (1772–1847) of 1806, and another by Daniel Maclise (1806–70) of 1831, both showing the artist at work. Neither of these can help to determine the authenticity of the work illustrated here. The *Portrait of John Constable, R. A., Aged Twenty* (1796) may be useful for comparison; although the shape of the nose is similar in both cases, the other features do not appear to have much in common.

Supposing it is a self-portrait, then it is interesting that Constable painted himself at all, particularly as there seems to be no attempt to surround himself with his attributes as an artist or to locate himself within a particular place or time. His eyes are prominent, as they are in the drawn self-portrait, although the drawing of 1806 shows him with a lot more hair. In this portrait, his hair is definitely receding, although the sideburns remain.

Never a portrait-painter by choice, Constable seems ill at ease with the shape of his face, his profile appearing almost lifeless, stern, and mask-like. The *chiaroscuro* effects of light and dark, however, work very well against the skin-tone of his forehead.

EPSOM VIEW (1809)

The Tate Gallery, London. Courtesy of AKG/

Erich Lessing

*C*ONSTABLE stayed with his uncle and aunt, James and Mary Gubbins, at Epsom several times, but notably in August 1806 and June 1809. It would seem that Constable observed the advice of friend and critic J. T. Smith about landscape painting. In this view from June 1809, there is an immediacy and sketchiness which appears to follow Smith's advice: "Do not set about inventing figures for a landscape taken from nature, for you cannot remain an hour in any spot, however solitary, without the appearance of some living thing that will in all probability accord better with the scene and time of day than will any invention of your own."

Here, the painting is brisk, the trees are abundant with leaves, and there is a pool of bright sunlight, which accentuates the hill and contrasts with the flat plain in the foreground. In the mid-ground, the lake interrupts the trees, drawing the eye onwards and upwards to the rest of the painting. The composition is almost two-thirds sky; the clouds appear to move swiftly across the scene, suggesting the transitory nature of the ever-changing sky contrasted with the permanence of the landscape itself.

FLATFORD LOCK AND MILL (1810–11)
Courtesy of Christie's Images

SEVERAL versions of this oil study exist; in this one a man is sitting by the lock. This sketch may have been painted for his maternal uncle, David Pike Watts, who desired a painting that would bear close scrutiny: "I do not want it for effect as in a place where I will hang it I cannot well retreat to a distance ... It must bear close examination."

The foliage and fauna painted in the foreground are carefully observed in dark greens, whites, and yellows. The mill house, to the left, is carefully detailed even at this stage in the series, although the mill itself is out of the picture. The man sitting at the edge of the lock in a bright-yellow waistcoat hangs on to one of the lock gates; he looks down and appears to dangle a stick into the water. To the left foreground, another figure in a red jacket kneels beside the sluice.

The line of the river runs up and through the picture. The trees act as a central axis around which the picture is built. At the second bend, the water disappears and the background opens into a rich vista, closed to the left by leafy trees but continuing and opening out to the right.

A LANDSCAPE NEAR EAST BERGHOLT: EVENING (1812)

Courtesy of the V & A Picture Library

THIS landscape, painted in the early evening on July 7 1812, portrays the cool of the evening after a bright summer's day. Constable wrote to his future wife, Maria Bicknell, on July 10 of that year, explaining why he was prompted to go out and paint in the evenings: " ... I am sure you will laugh when I tell you I have found another very promising subject at Flatford Mill. I do not study much abroad in the middle of these very hot bright days. I am become quite careful of myself, last year I almost put my eyes out by that pastime."

The edges of the painting have been tacked down around the edge of the stretcher, taking part of the foliage away and limiting the panoramic quality of the scene. This study is superb in its ability to depict the landscape in silhouette, as caused by the sun dropping behind the trees. The brush strokes are broad and sweeping and give just enough detail of the landscape and trees to make out where the scene is. The setting sun dominates as a white ball in relief, the paint thick, surrounded by a hue of yellow-pink.

In a landscape so familiar to the artist, the style is beautifully relaxed and un-self-conscious. The tree to the left sweeps into the picture plane, to meet a tree known to Constable as the "wig tree" because of its shape.

❋ A LANDSCAPE NEAR EAST BERGHOLT ❋

A HAYFIELD NEAR EAST BERGHOLT AT SUNSET (1812)

Courtesy of the V & A Picture Library

*T*HIS study was first painted on paper and laid on canvas at a later date.

Once again, Constable takes advantage of the fading light and coolness of the evening to study in paints a part of the country he already knew well. His attention to the scene is evident in the outlines of the shapes of the trees and the curves of the landscape. The sky becomes the background over which the landscape's silhouettes can be studied.

The foreground is dominated by hay rooks in a field that slopes down to the left. The undulating scene, when broken down into foreground, mid-ground, and background, becomes field, trees, and sky; a perfect horizontal composition that describes the effect the lowering sun has on the landscape's appearance.

The trees are not detailed, and yet they portray how a tree looks in the fading light. The hay takes on the tint of the sky, slightly pink-gray against the brown of the earth. The ricks are almost rock-like, yet there is enough to suggest the softness and density of hay to inform us that they are not rocks. The sky melts into red-pink tinged with blue-gray, which carries us out of the day in to evening.

PORCH OF EAST BERGHOLT CHURCH (C. 1810)

Courtesy of the V & A Picture Library

THIS oil sketch may have been in preparation for a finished work that is now lost. A painting now on show at the Tate Gallery in London shows a similar view, but it is not known whether this is a sketch for that painting. It has been suggested that the two paintings may be associated in some way, perhaps being executed at different times of day to show the changing light of daytime and evening, as with the views of *Dedham Vale* painted in 1802.

It is difficult to tell what is happening; whether the moon is rising or the sun setting, but it is getting dark and the scene will soon become obscured, with its features in silhouette. The church is drawn carefully in oil, and the porch is highlighted by the light of the moon or the setting sun. The white highlights on the porch, the people, and the patch of bright white glimpsed through the trees and on the gravestone nearest to the path all contrast with the dark-green of the trees and the reddening stone of the church building.

The sky is blue, on the point of turning to night, with white cloud and a hint of pink still visible. The tree in the center of the picture has already turned to a darkening mass, its green leaves turning slowly into a black silhouette.

DEDHAM MILL (C. 1810–15)
Courtesy of the V & A Picture Library

AN earlier version of this scene was sold at the British Institution in 1819, although this oil sketch on paper was probably made as a study for the painting *Dedham Lock and Mill* (1820). Constable probably returned to the painting in 1820 in the hope that he would make another sale.

The sketch is close to the painting sold in 1819 in that the foreground remains open with no evidence of the barge or the horse by the tree seen in the version of 1820. Dedham church seems to be the main focus in this sketch, and is less prominent in the later painting. Here, the trees on the right-hand side use a good portion of the picture and Constable attempts to enliven this area with some horses, reducing the foliage to show more of the surrounding ground. He was displeased with the emptiness of the foreground, and later added the barge to try to resolve this.

The sketch has a palette of gray, brown, and green with a little yellow and some white highlights, particularly on the water.

Dedham Lock and Mill (1820)
Courtesy of AKG Photo. (See p. 108)

A CART ON A LANE AT FLATFORD (1811)
Courtesy of the V & A Picture Library

SKETCHED from nature on May 16, 1811, this view of a lane leading to Flatford and is described as one of " ... the earliest dated oil sketches ... to show the full originality of Constable's mature style, its vivid naturalism of coloring and boldness of handling."

A horse and cart are just about to disappear round the bend in a lane. A bush, hedgerows, and trees obscure the bend, so that only the back of the cart and its driver, wearing a black hat, are visible. The track is burnt-orange in color, overlaid with white scratched on to the paint surface with a palette knife.

The left-hand side of the composition opens out to a flat lay-by that graduates up into a field. In the field are some grazing cows, their backs visible over the top of the hedge. Beyond the field, the landscape opens up into a lilac-blue expanse, edged with vibrant orange. On the far left is a house placed precariously on the edge of a hill.

Some crows fly over the fields, their silhouettes contrasting magically against the blue, white, and off-white of the sky. The scene is a riot of contrasting colors dominated by the strong orange against a spectrum of greens and lilac.

DEDHAM VALE (C. 1810)

Museo Lazaro Galdiano, Madrid. Courtesy of AKG Photo

THIS view of Dedham Vale, looking towards Langham church, is unusual for Constable in that it is so heavily populated. He seldom portrayed polite society in his landscapes, but here we have a perfect afternoon on what may be Sir William Godfrey's estate, with a group of three well-dressed middle-class people taking in the view. The woman with the parasol looks towards the gentleman's extended hand and their companion appears to listen to him intently as he talks. Three dogs play at the party's feet.

What the viewers see is, of course, something entirely different. We view the figures and the landscape from a higher viewpoint, along with the artist. Walking down the hill and away from the party is another female figure—by her dress, especially her shawl, she is likely to be someone who works on the estate.

The patchwork effect of the fields in the foreground, with their grazing cows and white sheep, begins to break towards the mid-ground, which is intercepted by trees and cottages. The light is golden, leading the eye down into the valley. The cottage to the right, with smoke rising from the chimney, has the same friendly familiarity as *Willy Lott's House with a Rainbow* (1820). The background opens into a recognizable view towards Langham, taking the viewer beyond the valley and away from Sir William's estate.

WILLY LOTT'S HOUSE,
NEAR FLATFORD MILL
(C. 1810–15)

Courtesy of the V & A Picture Library

*P*AINTED in a palette of dark green, brown, blue-gray, and white, this sombre sketch closely resembles the right-hand side of the sketch for *The Haywain* (1821). The sky is cloudy and gray, with thick impasto white laid on with a palette knife. The whitewash on the oblique edge of the cottage facing the pond is beautifully rendered, with sunlight shining through the clouds on to it and the leaves of the bush in front.

The black-and-white dog in the foreground is a familiar motif in Constable's work. Willy Lott's house is a similarly recognizable landmark to Constable, who grew up nearby. Clearly, *The Haywain*, painted in the studio, borrowed from several sketches that were painted outside from nature beforehand.

In this sketch, the view of the house is a different one to that illustrated in the sketch, *Willy Lott's House with a Rainbow* (1820). Here, the path goes from the right-hand corner up to the center-ground before curving away to the right again. The pond is in the middle, reflecting the landscape in its rippled surface. In *Willy Lott's House with a Rainbow*, the path is parallel to the picture plane.

***Willy Lott's House with a Rainbow* (c. 1820)**
Courtesy of Christie's Images. (See p. 110)

DEDHAM VALE: VIEW TO LANGHAM CHURCH (1811)

Weinberg Foundation, Switzerland. Courtesy of AKG Photo

PRESENTING Dedham Vale in quite a different mood to *Dedham Vale* (*c.* 1810), Constable collates the landscape around Dedham here in a familiar, although not particularly detailed way. The mature green of the foliage contrasts with the earthy red-ground in the foreground. The viewer is asked to examine the ground before taking in the wider, almost panoramic view.

The scene opens up into a patchwork of fields with grazing cows and horses punctuating the young, green, spring fields. In the neighboring field there appears to be a scarecrow, the ground looks just sown, quite bare and pale against the green field next to it.

In this sketch, Constable has begun to build up the background: the hills and plains, trees and cottages of the landscape he knew so well. The sky is an ominous mix of blue, white, and gray-brown, with the color of the buff paper showing through. The cloud formation suggests rain, and the light is softened, allowing for the contrasts in the greens, browns, reds, and off-whites of the landscape below it.

BARGES ON THE STOUR, WITH DEDHAM CHURCH IN THE DISTANCE (C. 1811)
Courtesy of the V & A Picture Library

*T*HE year 1811 was a breakthrough one for Constable, who handled his medium with a "vivid naturalism of coloring and boldness of handling" that was previously only implicit in his work. This moody, blue oil sketch on paper is similar to a later watercolor sketch, *View at Hampstead Looking Towards London* (1833).

Here, the blue is bright, emboldened by the yellow-white blaze burning through the otherwise somber sky. The soft gray-green of the grass is illuminated by the light falling on it. The few gray lines that delineate the lock gates, recognized as those near Flatford Mill, place the viewer in a particular landscape. In the foreground, the edge of the river fringes the bottom of the picture, a post and grass leads to the edge of the water. Here, a bright white denotes the light of the moon.

Constable's maternal uncle, David Pike Watts, wrote to him saying: "Cheerfulness is wanted in your landscapes; they are tinctured with a somber darkness." Constable was, indeed, heartbroken during this stay at Bergholt, as he was temporarily separated from his beloved Maria Bicknell, who was finally to become his wife in 1816.

MR GOLDING CONSTABLE'S HOUSE,
EAST BERGHOLT (C. 1811)
Courtesy of the V & A Picture Library

THE long panoramic view in this painting is not exceptional but it is interesting because it was painted from the garden of the house in which John Constable was born, as he records on the back of the canvas.

The detail of the architecture is not painted in, although the pilaster chimneys and stucco finish of the main house are drawn in. The high wall of what may be the garden is situated on the left; some

trees or bushes are visible above the top of the wall. The expanse of lawn in the foreground, with the suggestion of a fence and paddock, is flat and velvety. To the right, cows are grazing, possibly just let out from the barn that is on the right of the main house. The view is typically English, redolent of a gentle rural peace.

East Bergholt church can just be seen above the trees in the background on the left-hand side behind another house. The sky is gray-white, with a whisp of gray cloud on the far right of the painting.

LANDSCAPE WITH A
DOUBLE RAINBOW (1812)
Courtesy of the V & A Picture Library

THIS sketch of a double rainbow in oil on paper is an ecstatic representation of a phenomenon Constable later held to be artistically, spiritually, and religiously important. It is not until the 1830s that the rainbow took on a special significance for Constable, when he refers to it as a "mild arch of promise."

The sketch was painted from nature in East Bergholt, where Constable spent four months during the late summer and fall of 1812. His mood was sometimes melancholy as he was not financially secure enough to marry Maria Bicknell.

The view is from a low point among grass and bushes in the foreground. To the right a windmill can be glimpsed. The rainbow drops into the dark green bush on the left, while the other rainbow, horizontally curved behind it, disappears out of the edge of the picture. The central rainbow is painted red, white, and blue with the red muted against the dark sky and the latter two colors very bright. The second rainbow repeats the colors of the first in a more muted palette.

The grasses and central bush are golden-yellow, with brown and white highlights. Some shadowing in dark brown-black is dotted around beneath the bush. On the curve of the hill leading down into the valley is a highlight of yellowy-white, adding a dramatic horizontal line to complement the curved motif of the rainbows in the sky.

AUTUMNAL SUNSET (C. 1812)

Courtesy of the V & A Picture Library

*T*HIS oil sketch was originally started on paper and then stuck down on to a piece of canvas by the artist in order to extend the right and bottom edge of the composition. This improvisation seems to have an effect in the lower edge, in that the shaft of bright evening sunlight is extended down diagonally from the figure of the woman in the mid-ground.

An inscription indicates that the painting was engraved for Constable's sojourn into publishing for David Lucas's (1802–81) seminal publication, *English Landscape Scenery*. All the engravings, which were "edited" by Constable while in progress, seem to have caused him some anxiety, possibly because he found it difficult to have another artist translate his original sketches into a finished work in another medium.

An angry letter from Constable to David Lucas supports this belief. It states: "The Evening [*Autumnal Sunset*] is spoiled owing to your having fooled with the rooks—they were the chief feature—which caused me to adopt the subject— nobody knew what they are—but took them only for blemishes on the plate."

In the original sketch, the light is golden and the scene open and undulating. The rooks do, indeed, take center stage, flying off from the center of the picture away from the trees that enclose the vivid blue-green field at the bottom of the slope.

VIEW OF DEDHAM FROM THE LANE LEADING FROM EAST BERGHOLT CHURCH TO FLATFORD (C. 1810–15)

Courtesy of the V & A Picture Library

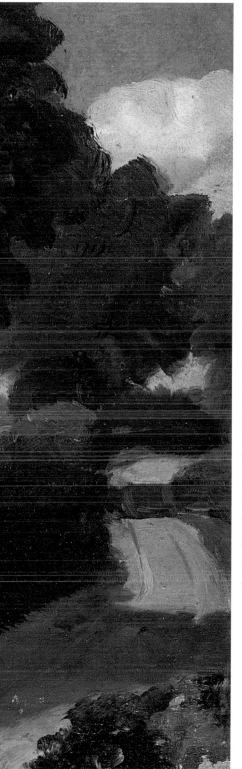

*A*MODERNISTIC composition of flat areas of color and an unusually gentle sky, this oil sketch is comparable in style to two other works. There is a formal similarity with *A Cart on the Lane at Flatford* (1811) and, more imaginatively perhaps, with *Study of Tree Trunks* (1821), for its sweeping path, boundaries of hedges and trees, and attention to shadow.

The view looks over the hedge towards Dedham and down the lane towards Flatford. The hedge, appearing at first in the bottom left-hand corner, shows very dark-brown ground and little green. It sweeps into the picture, making way for the lane that follows the same horizontal curve, before turning to the right.

The first tree interrupts the top of the hedge, breaks up the sky and casts a shadow on the lane. The next tree does the same; as it brightens, the green contrasts with the orange of the field to the left. Looking beyond the field, a blue river meanders through the countryside. A line of yellow briefly interrupts, catching the eye, before it sweeps the skyline. The sky is a soft blue with white cloud falling on to the horizon. The cloud graduates from left to right to converge with the bend in the lane, the sweep of the hedge, the top of the tree, and the ultimate vanishing point within the picture.

LOCK ON THE STOUR (C. 1813)
Courtesy of Christie's Images

*T*HIS oil study may be the study for *Landscape: Lock on the Stour*, bought by James Carpenter at the British Institution in 1814. It is brilliantly composed from a series of sweeping, sketchy brush-strokes and rich, golden colors.

The viewpoint is microscopic in its attention to the detail in the foreground foliage, resembling closely the work of Jacob van Ruisdael, the Dutch 17th-century landscape painter. Constable's focus is very much on the ground, with the boys' weight positioned firmly on the bank, their bodies and all their attention concentrated on the activity of fishing from the lock. The focus of this painting might be better understood by considering the 18th-century idea of absorption. The boys are completely absorbed in their fishing; while the artist portrays this, he is asking his viewer to become absorbed in the beauty and variety of the scene itself.

The water sloshes through the sluice—streaks of white depict the transience of rushing water superbly. The foliage around the lock is dark green, burnt orange, and white, while the sweeping tree to the left frames the picture. The tree touches the sky, which is heavily built up from thick white, blue, and pink. The thatched cottage, which is accessed by the bridge, brings the viewer back around the path to the foreground gravel and the boys.

LOCK ON THE STOUR ❋

A WOODED LANDSCAPE OUTSIDE THE PARK PALES OF OLD HALL, EAST BERGHOLT, WITH A PLOUGHMAN (1814)

Courtesy of Christie's Images

CONSTABLE exhibited this painting in 1814 at the Royal Academy. John Allnutt, a London wine merchant, bought it either at the exhibition or shortly afterwards. Allnutt asked artist John Linnell (1792–1882) to paint over the sky, but was not pleased with the outcome and asked Constable to repaint the sky and reduce the size of the canvas. Rather than do this, Constable painted another version of the painting.

The painting here is the first version. The view is from outside the Old Hall, East Bergholt, where Sir William Godfrey lived. The painting was accompanied at the Royal Academy exhibition by several lines from Robert Bloomfield's (1766–1823) *The Farmer's Boy* ("Spring", lines 71-72), where the emphasis is on work:

"But unassisted through each toilsome day,
With smiling brow the ploughman cleaves his way."

The scene is familiar, but the emphasis is on the two men ploughing. The ploughmen were a later addition to the landscape. As Constable noted, "I have added some ploughmen to the landscape from the park pales, which is a great help, but I must try and warm the picture a little more if I can ... it is bleak and looks as if there would be a shower of sleet, and that you know is too much the case with my things."

A WINDMILL AT STOKE, NEAR IPSWICH (1814)

Courtesy of the V & A Picture Library

THIS pen and watercolor sketch designed by Constable for an engraving by John Landseer (1769–1852), is similar in view to *A Windmill Near Brighton* (1828), although the two contrast brilliantly in their handling; this is in pen and watercolor, the other in paint laid on thick with a palette knife; and this version is concerned with the landscape, while the other is only concerned with the light on the windmill.

In *A Windmill at Stoke*, two cows are lying in the field adjacent to the mill. The land slopes to show a figure riding down the path in a horse-drawn cart, while coming up the hill is a figure carrying a spade. The landscape pans out to the right depicting a church in the distance.

The palette of green, red-brown, sepia, and mauve is muted. The light is of a fresh winter morning. Constable has used a sepia pen to draw the outlines of the horse and cart and the windmill, the wooden body and paddles of which contrasted well with the domed brick storehouse. A shadow on the field just in front of the cows which is cast by the paddles of the windmill, is a turquoise and mauve mix, reflecting both the trees around the mill and the sky.

STUDY OF FLOWERS IN A HYACINTH GLASS (1814)
Courtesy of the V & A Picture Library

*I*NSCRIBED on the back: "South Kensington Museum Flowers painted by John Constable R. A.", this flower study is signed and dated July 26 by the artist, but the year cannot be read due to deterioration of the millboard on which it is painted.

The flower study is influenced by the work of the Flemish flower-piece painter Jan Brueghel (1568–1625) and his follower, Nicholaes van Verendael (1640–91), but is comparatively awkwardly painted and unaccomplished. However, Constable was aware that the Flemish flower-piece genre relied on absolute precision in detail and accuracy of color, and he attempted to emulate the style slavishly. He also paid close attention to the techniques of the Dutch landscape painter Jacob van Ruisdael.

The vase is central to the composition, with a highlight on its front top edge. It holds a haphazard arrangement of English garden flowers, with some greenery to add volume to the display. The light, coming from the right, highlights the arrangement while leaving the left-hand side of the composition in comparative shade.

Study of Foliage (c. 1820–30)
Courtesy of the V & A Picture Library. (See p. 118)

STUDY OF FLOWERS IN A GLASS VASE (C. 1814)

Courtesy of the V & A Picture Library

CONSTABLE was not an accomplished still-life painter but he was adept at observing nature closely. He showed a great sensibility towards composition, *chiaroscuro* and color and these still lives hold an important place within the ephemera that he sketched throughout his career.

This study resembles *Study of Flowers in a Hyacinth Glass* (1814). It appears to be a similar vase of flowers, this time with more blooms of a similar variety, and painted at South Kensington Museum in London. The vase has a highlight on the center of the rim, and the light comes from the left. The rubbery dark-green leaves on the left-hand side shine. The palette includes more yellow and blue than *Study of Flowers in Hyacinth Glass* and the arrangement is more haphazard. Snaking off to the right is a stalk of greenery, which floats into dark shadow.

Chiaroscuro plays a large part in the study. Painted on a dark background, the left-hand side reveals brown; on the right it is nearly black. On the left, the colors of the flowers are more intense. In the center of the vase there is a white flower that catches the light. Beyond this bloom, the display begins to recede into darkness, the colors become more subdued and the outlines less defined.

Study of Flowers in a Hyacinth Glass (1814)
Courtesy of the V & A Picture Library. (See p. 88)

BOAT-BUILDING NEAR FLATFORD MILL (1815)
Courtesy of the V & A Picture Library

THIS splendid painting, exhibited at the Royal Academy in 1815, is an industrious scene set in a Claudian landscape. Painted in the open air, executed with a great deal of care in meticulous detail and to a high level of "finish", it is not a hastily painted sketch.

The "finish" apparent in this painting may be attributed to the advice given to Constable by a colleague, Joseph Farington (1747–1821), which led him to go and look at the Angerstein pictures by Claude Lorrain: " ... before he returns to his country studies, and to attend to the admirable manner in which all the parts of his pictures are completed ...." Constable evidently took this advice, making a picture with all the "finish" of Claude and borrowing from the master's *Seaport with the Embarcation of St Ursula* in subject-matter and composition.

It was said by a friend of the artist that: "This perfect work remained in his [Constable's] possession to the end of his life." A reason for Constable's attachment to the painting may be its subject matter: a barge under construction in his father's boat yard near Flatford Mill.

SCENE ON A NAVIGABLE RIVER (FLATFORD MILL) (1816–17)
The Tate Gallery, London. Courtesy of AKG/Erich Lessing

THE period 1816–21 marks a change in Constable's working habits following his eventual marriage to Maria Bicknell. This painting, generally known as *Flatford Mill,* was the first in a series of large 6-ft (1.8-m) canvases painted in the studio and drawn from sketches made around the Stour Valley. *Flatford Mill* was exhibited at the Royal Academy in 1817, but it failed to sell. Following this, Constable appears to have reworked it slightly, repainting the foliage on the large tree to the right and most of the smaller tree behind it.

It is a nostalgic work, painted from a slightly elevated viewpoint, looking towards the southern end of the footbridge at Flatford. The mill buildings can be seen in the background, while to the left barges are being untied from the towing-horse to be poled under the bridge. The boy twists his body around to watch as the men unharness the horse, his small frame in harmony with the huge workhorse upon which he sits. Another boy pulls in the rope.

The scene is painted in minute detail: the foliage and trees, the dusty path, the water ebbing with the flow of the tide, and the men doing the heavy work. The horse's shadow lingers, the day is still, the trees stand motionless and smoke comes out of the chimney in an idle stream. On the green to the right of the picture, birds fly down to pick worms from the wet grass and the clouds portend rain.

COAST SCENE NEAR OSMINGTON,
WITH PORTLAND ISLAND IN THE DISTANCE (1816)
Courtesy of the V & A Picture Library

ON October 2, 1816, Constable finally married Maria Bicknell. His good friend, the Reverend John Fisher, both officiated at the wedding and then invited the couple to spend their honeymoon with him and his wife at their vicarage in Osmington in Dorset. The prospect was described by Fisher as: "wonderfully wild and sublime and well worth a painter's visit."

This pencil and watercolor sketch was made during Constable's six-week stay in Dorset, which gave him his first experience of rugged and dramatic coastline, of cliffs, rocks, the shore, and spectacular coastal light. The work of the early 1800s in the Lake District, for example *Taylor Ghyll, Sty Head, Borrowdale* (1806), may be compared with the output of this brief period. Both have similar force of expression in the way elements in nature exist: the water against the land or rock, the sea against the sky, the light and how it reacts on the landscape, and on the landscape itself.

Here, the sea shimmers, lapping a rocky shore on which there is a little boat shored up. There is sand, too, suggested by a soft beige wash. In the background, Portland Island can be seen, blue-gray against a pink-gray sky.

791.'88

WEYMOUTH BAY (1816)
Courtesy of the V & A Picture Library

*T*HIS is one of about 20 drawings and several oil sketches that occupied the artist while he and his wife Maria stayed with his long-time friend, the Reverend John Fisher on their honeymoon in Dorset. The friendship with Fisher was an enduring one: "Believe—my very dear Fisher, I should almost faint by the way when I am standing before my large canvasses was I not cheered and encouraged by your friendship and approbation."

This may be the earliest work (of three) by Constable painted at Weymouth Bay—there is debate about which of the three Weymouth Bay paintings (one at the National Gallery, London, one at the Louvre in Paris and this at the Victoria and Albert Museum, London) is the earliest.

Painted in the open air from nature, the oil portrays a beautiful romantic vision of a moonlit but stormy night at Weymouth Bay. Two figures are on the beach: a woman with a parasol and a man, their clothes swept by the wind. A rocky cliff climbs up the right-hand edge of the picture, sheltering the two figures in its shadow. A magnificent pool of blue-white water graduates into dark until it appears white again on the skyline. The sky is very dark, enclosing the scene in a shroud of darkness with the merest streaks of light.

ON THE THAMES NEAR BATTERSEA BRIDGE (C. 1816)

Courtesy of Christie's Images

AFTER 1816, following his marriage to Maria Bicknell, Constable became a Londoner. Away from East Anglia and the landscape that was so familiar to him, like many of his contemporaries he explored the river Thames with its extraordinary light, virulent tides, bridges, buildings, and foreshore.

In this oil sketch, painted at high tide from the north bank of the river, a large, rather clumsy barge is silhouetted on the tidal water and dominates the mid-ground, while the foreground is murky-dark and lightless. The sky against the water is startling—the sketchy clouds break to allow a shaft of light, which shines down on to the water to contrast against the choppy, almost sinister darkness of the water in the foreground of the picture.

On the south side of the Thames, Battersea Mill, a veritable tower of white, looms over the Thames beneath the cloudy sky. The flecks of white so often used in Constable's landscape painting are dominant in this view; they skip across the water and flit through the sky.

HOUSES AT PUTNEY HEATH (1818)

Courtesy of the V & A Picture Library

*I*N the summer of 1818 Constable made several visits to Louisa House, the house that his father-in-law Charles Bicknell rented in Putney following the death of his wife. Constable's own wife Maria stayed there several times, and was on one occasion accompanied by their small son. Constable, meanwhile, continued to work at his London studio in Keppel Street. It was on one visit to Putney, on August 13, 1818, that he executed this beautiful watercolor drawing, of which there are three similar versions.

It is conceivable that the three delicately drawn and colored watercolors were made for each of the Bicknell sisters as gifts. This may

explain their intimate quality and finished, postcard-like appearance.
Here, the view is wide and panoramic. The heath looks dusty-dry and
the colors are almost that of a desert.

Louisa House stands to the left of the painting, and it appears
almost fortress-like on the parched heath in the hot summer month
of August. The pale blue-gray of the slate roof on the main house is
matched perfectly with the color of the summer sky. The blue of
the sky against the green of the trees is not rich, but a washed-out
Mediterranean tone, soaked with strong summer light. The heath seems
to be be deserted, but the house appears to be lived-in—well and truly
inhabited by the Bicknell family.

BRANCH HILL POND, HAMPSTEAD (1819)

Courtesy of the V & A Picture Library

*T*HIS is the first oil sketch that Constable made of Branch Hill Pond, Hampstead, which was later to act as a template for several studies and finished paintings.

The horses and cow drinking on the left of the picture are motifs that often appear in Constable's work. One of the horses still has its mount, represented by a red dash. The red dash, like white, seems to be a recurring shorthand device for depicting transience and, in contrast to the landscape, objects that do not remain constant.

This is a cloudy fall day in England when the sky and mist close in and the light has almost no opacity. Outside, Hampstead Heath feels hostile; the light is dull and imposing. The sky to the left is heavy; the white paint is laid on very thickly. The gray cloud shrouds the horizon in heavy mist, closing off the vista with an ethereal thud. The ripples on the pond give the water a cold-gray temperament.

The rocky, mossy bank on the right similarly restricts the view, forcing the eye down it to the center of the composition and the pond, to follow the curving line of the landscape beyond, before meeting the impenetrable cloud.

THE OPENING OF WATERLOO BRIDGE
FROM WHITEHALL STAIRS: JUNE 18TH, 1817 (1819)
Courtesy of the V & A Picture Library

THERE are several studies in pencil and oil that relate to the finished painting of the ceremonial of the opening of Waterloo Bridge, London, exhibited finally by Constable in 1832. The studies from life may have been made at the time of the ceremony, seen from the upstairs window of No. 5 Whitehall Yard on the Embankment.

G.R. Rennie's Waterloo Bridge was opened by the Prince Regent on June 18, 1817 (the bridge was demolished in 1936). No other work caused Constable so much trouble and anxiety, but he pursued it as a worthy subject for exhibition. He would persist with the subject only to become disheartened and give it up; then pick it up again only to drop it once again. The process was repeated at least four times, which is why there are so many versions of the picture.

This sketch, busy with red, white, and black, is compositionally quite different from the final painting. The terrace on the left becomes a bow-fronted house and the Embankment, here obscured by trees, is better defined. Waterloo Bridge and St Paul's Cathedral remain in the background, as does the activity in the mid-ground, including the barges and general chaos of the event.

DEDHAM LOCK AND MILL (1820)

V & A Museum, London. Courtesy of AKG Photo

THIS is probably the last of three versions of *Dedham Lock and Mill*. Dedham Mill was one of the watermills worked by Constable's father and then, following his death in 1816, looked after by his brother Abram. It is possible that he painted another two versions of the subject, hoping to repeat the success of *A Mill* (1819), which was sold at exhibition. The third version of 1820 is very similar to this one.

This is busier than the version of 1819; the boat is in the left foreground, and there are grazing horses in front of the tree to the right. Constable has used white flecks to denote the movement of the water that cascades down the steps into the reservoir; flecks of white on the mill wheel suggest its turning action—lifting the water and dropping it again. The wavering of the trees is also expressed by white paint. The smoke from the chimney of the mill floats up at a slight angle; there is movement in the air.

In the mid-ground a man ties up a barge, while two more figures walk towards the viewer on the left-hand side of the mill house. Dedham church is seen in the background, drawing the eye to the center of the composition and its overall symmetry.

WILLY LOTT'S HOUSE WITH A RAINBOW (C. 1820)

Courtesy of Christie's Images

*T*WO of Constable's major motifs—obsessions almost—are combined in this sketch. Both are used in major exhibited works, as well as appearing in sketches and drawings, becoming an integral part of his visual language. Willy Lott's house becomes central to *The Haywain* (*c.* 1821), and the rainbow motif is used in a painting of Salisbury and in the work based on Stonehenge.

The rainbow in this sketch in red, white, and blue, arches down into the center of the picture plane, disappearing behind a tree. Willy Lott's Suffolk house, sketched hastily in long, sweeping strokes, stands obliquely against the path where a cow saunters lazily across the midground. The reflections of both the house and the animal are suggested in the stream, which is barely represented. The canvas is visible around the edges of the sketch, although no ground is visible through the paint, except around the roof of the house.

The strokes of paint, although swift and flat, are brash with confident coloring. The composition works well, relying on the sweep of the diagonal rainbow, the oblique of the house, the trees, and the path, and the triangles created by the roof of the house and the lawn in front of it.

**Willy Lott's House, Near Flatford Mill
(c. 1810–15)**
Courtesy of the V & A Picture Library.
(See p. 68)

SALISBURY CATHEDRAL WITH ARCHDEACON FISHER'S HOUSE SEEN FROM THE RIVER (1820)
Courtesy of AKG/Erich Lessing

*T*HIS oil sketch of John Fisher's house, seen from the opposite bank of the river, was probably painted in mid- to late-August 1820, when Constable visited his friend, by now an archdeacon with his wife and two children. He made a number of drawings and oil sketches during this visit, including *Scene on a River Near Salisbury* and *A Road Leading to Salisbury*, plus two further studies of the cathedral itself and the close.

This oil study has a tremendously energetic and happy tone. The light is bright, accentuated by the red, gray, and yellowy-white ground, the sketchiness of which allows us to see Constable's working of the sky to highlight the whites so beautifully. The riverbank is busy with people strolling and sitting under trees and on benches.

The red dashes create an energetic, carnival feel. Perhaps it is a Sunday after the service at the cathedral. Archdeacon Fisher's house is seen from the side—hardly visible—on the bank of the river, dwarfed by the cathedral and surrounded by the monumental trees of the Cathedral grounds.

Salisbury Cathedral from the South-West (1820)
Courtesy of the V & A Picture Library. (See p. 116)

SALISBURY CATHEDRAL AND THE CLOSE (1820)
Courtesy of the V & A Picture Library

THERE would have been nothing but praise about the sky and Constable's use of light and shade in this painting. This oil sketch appears to be unrelated to any finished exhibited work.

The painting shows the spire of the cathedral stretching up into a blue summer sky. Painted in August 1820, the flowerbeds are full of blooms and the trees are green, one tree casts a shadow on the lawn, the others gently surround the cathedral. In the foreground, the sandy path leads the eye into the picture to the mid-ground among the trees and flowers of the close. The spindly architecture of the cathedral contrasts with the gentle contours of the surrounding trees. The left of the painting is in comparative shadow to contrast with the bright summer light of the central feature of the cathedral.

Constable's palette comprised of soft contrasts of the blue-and-white of the sky against the stone-and-white architecture of the cathedral. The trees, grass, and flowers are his signature; a number of greens darkened and lightened by black and white.

SALISBURY CATHEDRAL FROM THE SOUTH-WEST (1820)
Courtesy of the V & A Picture Library

SALISBURY Cathedral was a favorite subject of Constable's. This painting is similar in style to *Salisbury Cathedral and the Close* (1820). It is probable that both sketches, painted on the same visit to Salisbury to see Archdeacon John Fisher, were executed outside in the open air.

The close is not in view in this version of Salisbury Cathedral. Instead, a larger part of the cathedral itself comes right out beyond the center of the picture. The architecture and fenestration, which gave Constable some trouble, are painted as though melting like a giant decorative candle.

Here, the spire of the cathedral disappears out of the picture, as in the other sketch. The sky is now more dramatic; palette of gray-pink, white, and blue, heavily painted. The trees, which are beautifully painted, are cleverly back-lit by the white cloud and in contrast with the blue of the sky and the yellow stone of the cathedral. Some cows are grazing in the park while a group of people wander around the cathedral, possibly sightseeing or coming out of a church service.

STUDY OF FOLIAGE (C. 1820–30)

Courtesy of the V & A Picture Library

CONSTABLE'S studies for foliage, flowers, trees, and clouds are an important part of his repertoire as a painter of nature. This study of foliage has not been identified as appearing in any work, although it has affinities with the foreground compositions of several of the large Stour Valley paintings, notably *The Leaping Horse* (1825).

This study, painted in oil on blue paper, initiates a dark, somber contemplation of leaves, probably dock leaves. The background of dark, rich brown has a yellow highlight in the bottom right-hand corner. The leaves are positioned growing out of the right-hand corner of the paper, and are painted the rich, dark green of shade-loving plants.

The study may have been painted in the studio, using nature-study pieces that Constable had collected specifically for the purpose. The critic W. P. Frith, R. A. (1819–1909) relates in *My Autobiography and Reminiscences* (1888) an occasion when, on visiting Constable in his studio, the artist told him: " ... never do anything without nature before you, if it be possible to have it ... I know dock-leaves pretty well, but I should not attempt to introduce them into a picture without having them before me."

HAMPSTEAD HEATH (1820–30)
Courtesy of the V & A Picture Library

THIS view towards Highgate is a finished oil, and was possibly exhibited at the Royal Academy in 1822. There is no certainty in this, although in a letter to his friend, Archdeacon John Fisher, Constable refers to a painting of "Green Highgate."

The landscape is green and fertile. The paths meander through the undulating landscape with people walking in several directions and about to converge in the center of the composition. In the left foreground some mules are grazing, and a couple of fowl rummage on the ground. Several daubs of vivid red suggest the garments of the walkers dotted here and there throughout the landscape.

The people walking appear to be middle-class and out for a stroll. Walking up the path, past the mules, is a boy who probably works in the grounds. The woman and the two children on the path have a bicycle. The light is bright, the air still and the sky a perfect summer blue with a few scattered clouds. The water of the pond reflects the sky and the light. In the distance, on Squire's Mount, is Kenwood House.

FLATFORD OLD BRIDGE AND BRIDGE COTTAGE ON THE STOUR (C. 1820–30)

Courtesy of the V & A Picture Library

*T*HIS drawing, made in pencil, pen, brown ink, and wash, is probably composed from drawings made in 1813. The footbridge and cottage at Flatford appear time and again in Constable's work throughout his career. Despite this repetition, the atmosphere of each picture alters depending on what he decides to accentuate, what time of day it is and the medium he chooses.

This view, with the semblance of a rainbow above the cottage, is hastily drawn and suggests a somewhat restless mood. It is quite intense in its use of black and highlights of brown. The white of the paper is employed to represent the white of the light, creating the light and dark contrasts that Constable used to express "... one brief moment caught from fleeting time."

Two figures are walking across the bridge, while a barge floats beneath them. A small dog in the foreground runs out of the composition on the right. The trees on the right-hand side can be seen in *Flatford Mill* (1816–17) and associated drawings and sketches. Here, Constable has inserted them from imagination, for they do not exist in this spot by the bridge but are downstream.

MALVERN HALL, WARWICKSHIRE (1821)

Tesse Museum, Le Mans. Courtesy of AKG/Erich Lessing

CONSTABLE visited Malvern Hall twice and this landscape of 1821 is one of three paintings of the subject, which are all very similar; two with the peacocks and one without.

Malvern Hall was the seat of Henry Greswold Lewis (1754–1829). He employed Constable on various occasions, and although it appears that the artist was not always enthusiastic about the commissions offered (they included several portraits and copies), financially he was in no position to refuse. Lewis wrote to Constable in 1819: "Malvern is going on and is much improved inside and out and would make a much better figure in landscape than when you painted it last."

Despite Constable's ambivalence, Malvern Hall had indeed seen some changes. Here he makes a point of showing the newly built balustraded terrace at the front of the house and a pair of gate piers that were based on a design by Inigo Jones. The oblique view of the house allows Constable to place the subject within a landscape that shows Solihull Church in the background, while in the foreground, bathed in a pool of light from the west, is a peacock.

BUILDINGS ON RISING GROUND
NEAR HAMPSTEAD (1821)
Courtesy of the V & A Picture Library

*T*HE inscription on this sketch, almost certainly painted outside, describes the time of day and weather conditions. The date is 13 October, 1821, the time between four and five in the afternoon, and it was "very fine with gentle wind at N.E."

The sky is sketchy, but the clouds on the horizon are melting on to the horizon, beyond The Salt Box, a name for this house on Branch Hill Pond. The sketch seems to be also concerned with the general topography of the area, viewed from a distance on low ground.

It is interesting to note the way in which the sketch is composed, horizontally across the picture plane, with the yellow-green of the foreground intercepted by the sky-blue of the pond, punctuated once again by the yellow-green of the hill and then by blue again. The composition is contained by the dark greens and browns to the left of the bushes and trees, which send the pond into shadow, and to the right, by the hue of gray-blue on the hill. The whites and the chalky grays delineate the paths, the house, the smoke, boulders, stones, and rocks.

TREES AT HAMPSTEAD:
THE PATH TO CHURCH (1821)
Courtesy of the V & A Picture Library

***Taylor Ghyll, Sty Head, Borrowdale* (1806)**
Courtesy of the V & A Picture Library.
(See p. 42)

HAMPSTEAD Parish Church is barely visible through the trees on the extreme left of this wonderful portrait composition painted by Constable in September 1821. The painting was bequeathed to the Victoria and Albert Museum in London by Isabel Constable, who had described the painting thus: "The upright and large picture of *Trees at Hampstead* which is sometimes called *The Path to Church.*"

This painting may have been exhibited at the Royal Academy in 1822, entitled *A Study of Trees from Nature.* Almost certainly painted in the open air, the composition is wonderful. The trees stretch up to the sky, bent and majestic. Light throws up shadows on the lower bark of the first tree on the left. The leaves are painted intricately, wavering on their branches against the sky. The trees, described by Constable as "Ashes, Elms, and Oaks etc ...", create a mid-ground composition which forces the eye upwards towards the sky. The sky is blue behind the white-gray September clouds, the blue showing through only occasionally. As a study in landscape, this is considerably detailed in comparison with earlier works such as *Taylor Ghyll, Sty Head, Borrowdale* (1806).

STUDY OF SKY AND TREES (C. 1821)
Courtesy of the V & A Picture Library

*U*NLIKE the later cloud studies, this study of sky and trees has a substantial fringe of grass, flowers, bushes, and trees in the lower half. There is no inscription by the artist on the back of the paper, but the work is thought to predate his other cloud studies. This sketch may therefore belong with a group of sky and tree studies made by Constable in Hampstead in 1821.

The viewpoint for this study is very low; we are seeing the ground, not just the tops of the trees as they meet the sky. In the foreground wild flowers and grasses graduate into bushes, which conceal the bottom parts of the trees. The palette is a remarkable mixture of greens, ranging from yellow-green to the blue-gray-green of the leaves where all color has almost disappeared, turned dark with the sunless sky above them.

The sky, painted in a thin blue oil with the paper visible beneath it, is gradually built up in swirling waves of white, gray, and an intense blue. Almost at the center of the composition is a burst of green-gray with the consistency of watercolor, which may have been created by a heavy drop of rain falling on the oil paint and paper while Constable worked.

VIEW IN A GARDEN WITH
A RED HOUSE BEYOND (C. 1821)
Courtesy of the V & A Picture Library

*L*argely due to its emphasis on the sky, it is thought that this study may belong with the series of sky and tree studies that Constable made while living at No. 2 Lower Terrace, Hampstead, London. The study is comparable to *The Grove, or Admiral's House, Hampstead* (*c*. 1821–22).

Here, we have a tree-filled rear view of the houses in Lower Terrace. The painting may have been composed from one of the top-floor windows at this address which Constable and his family rented for a time. The view looks out across the treetops to a red house in the background. On the right is a washing line with clothes pegged on to it, fluttering in the wind. Visually, the motif works beautifully: the white clothes, entering the picture diagonally, contrast with the green, yellow, and brown of the trees.

The clothes hanging among a forest of trees divert the eye from the central horizontal axis of the picture, drawing the eye over to the right towards the red house. The house, with just the roof and attic windows visible, has smoke coming from its chimneys against a rapidly graying sky. Two large fir trees dominate the skyline to the right of the chimney.

The Grove, or Admiral's House, Hampstead (c. 1821–22)
Courtesy of the V & A Picture Library. (See p. 144)

STUDY OF TREE TRUNKS (*C.* 1821)

Courtesy of the V & A Picture Library

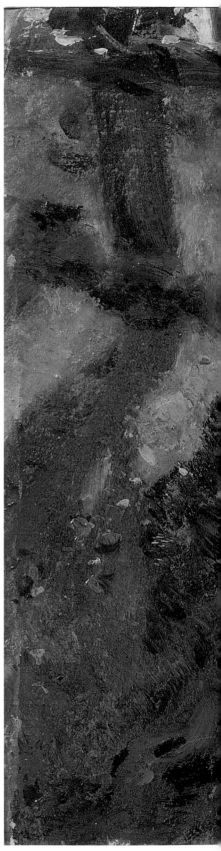

*T*HIS study, probably produced during the period when Constable was making his cloud and tree studies in Hampstead, is dated around 1821, although stylistically, it has an affinity with his later work.

The artist appears to be at the top of a mound on which two trees stand, although only a part of their trunks is visible. The roots of the foreground tree, drawn with swift strokes of brown, gray, green, and yellow, claw the bank, which is cast in shadow. The second tree in the distance is undefined, more plausible for its long shadow cast by the late sun than for the rendering of its trunk. It is evening, a time we know Constable favored for practical as well as artistic reasons.

A branch hangs down decoratively over the path, inviting the eye downwards to where a figure is standing. No sky is visible; the focus is on the ground, at the tree's roots, and on the figure exiting at the top right-hand corner. To balance with this directional focus, the roots of the tree spread out towards the bottom left-hand corner of the painting. The light effects in the two corners are in opposition, however —the figure in sunlight and the tree's roots in shadow.

Study of the Trunk of an Elm Tree (c. 1821)
Courtesy of the V & A Picture Library. (See p. 136)

STUDY OF THE TRUNK OF AN ELM TREE (C. 1821)

Courtesy of the V & A Picture Library

*T*HIS study of a tree trunk is similar to the series of carefully
studied clouds and trees produced by Constable in Hampstead
during 1821. The almost photographic quality of the trunk of
the central tree is extraordinary, even for an artist as attentive to nature
and sensitive to light, color, and texture as Constable was.

Constable's debt to the Dutch landscapists and, in particular, to
Jacob van Ruisdael, cannot be over-emphasized. Here, the tree trunk
stands in the center of the painting, lopped off as its branches reach out
for the sky. The bark is elephantine in texture and painted with a range
of earth colors, including brown, black, gray, green, yellow, and some
white. Soft, green, velvety moss creeps up the bark. A knarled knot can
be seen on the left about two-thirds of the way up the trunk. The lower
branches pirouette, twisting and turning and reaching out in to the
background, out of sight.

In the background,
the trees are represented in a
familiar Constable style,
painted in a palette of
green, yellow, and white.
Beyond the trees is a house.
The lawn holds a pool of
golden light into which a
bird momentarily hops.

Study of Sky and Trees (c. 1821)
*Courtesy of the V & A Picture
Library. (See p. 130)*

FULL-SIZE STUDY FOR
THE HAYWAIN (C. 1821)
Courtesy of the V & A Picture Library / K.F. Jackson.

*T*HIS is a full-scale study for *The Haywain* (1821), and is painted on a large 6-ft (1.8-m) canvas. It belongs with the group of paintings of Stour Valley subjects. *The White Horse* (1819) is the first of the sequence, all of which made use of sketches from the open air and were then painted in the studio.

Willy Lott's house, by now a familiar motif, is on the left, surrounded by trees. Constable did not have a suitable sketch for the wagon and that is why it appears so undefined here. For the finished painting in which the wagon is painted with more definition, he employed a friend's son, Johnny Dunthorne, to sketch one for him.

In the foreground of this sketch, a small boy on a barge horse waits at the water's edge; both were painted out of the final picture. The black and white dog on the bank is borrowed from previous compositions. The dog remains in the final composition, alone on the bank and turned parallel to the water's edge. The sky is an ominous gray above the trees on the left, while dark cloud enters the picture from the top right-hand corner.

Willy Lott's House, near Flatford Mill (c. 1810–15)
Courtesy of the V & A Picture Library. (See p. 68)

VIEW IN A GARDEN,
WITH A SHED ON THE LEFT (C. 1821)
Courtesy of the V & A Picture Library

THIS sketch may be another view overlooking the gardens at Lower Terrace, Hampstead, where Constable and his family rented No. 2 in 1821. In order that he could spend more time with his family, he made a makeshift studio in the coal shed in the back garden. He also painted looking out of the upper windows of the house —as in *View in a Garden with a Red House Beyond* (*c.* 1821) and *The Grove, or Admiral's House, Hampstead* (*c.* 1821–22).

Given that he was preoccupied during this time with a plethora of studies for the sky and trees, Constable's output during 1821 was impressive. He took the subjects for his sketches from a variety of very ordinary, everyday things. The building on the left may be the coal shed, although there is no evidence to support this. The "shed" is butted up to the left-hand side of the picture, the roof jutting out diagonally to meet a stone garden wall over which we look towards the background trees. The trees, painted brown, green, yellow, and black, both contrast and complement the color of the horizontal wooden slats visible on the sides of the coal shed.

The sky, light in color behind the trees, graduates to light gray, pink, and then an incredible swirling mass of dark gray-black that hugs both sides of the picture. The white wooden slats at the top of the shed reflect what is left of the sun. Below, seen through the window, there may be a figure, indicated by a red dash.

The Grove, or Admiral's House, Hampstead (c. 1821–22)
Courtesy of the V & A Picture Library.
(See p. 144)

BRANCH HILL POND, HAMPSTEAD (C. 1821–22)

Courtesy of the V & A Picture Library

CONSTABLE and his family rented a house in Hampstead for the summer of 1821. He had painted this same subject in 1819 when he first went to live in Hampstead. The heath and its environs were to offer him much in terms of an artistic atmosphere and the opportunity to work from nature.

Branch Hill Pond, Hampstead instigated Constable's career as a painter in London. He never again spent protracted periods in his native Suffolk, although he still visited, and his sojourns to various places to see colleagues, patrons, and friends provide a diary of drawings and sketches throughout his career.

There are several versions of *Branch Hill Pond Hampstead* dating from 1819, but this sketch, painted in 1821–22, opens out into a vista that only the flat heath could offer. The greens, browns, white, and ochres of the Suffolk and Salisbury work are replaced by a cooler palette, similar to that expressed in the watercolors made in Putney in 1818. The heath during the summer was a pale, sandy, dry color, the sky a cool gray-blue, and the light unforgiving and stark: there is no warmth in this sketch except for the dash of red earth in the foreground.

THE GROVE, OR ADMIRAL'S HOUSE, HAMPSTEAD (C. 1821–22)

Courtesy of the V & A Picture Library

*T*HIS painting and *View in a Garden with a Red House Beyond* (*c.* 1821) are Constable at his most "domestic". Unusually, in this painting Constable is describing the back of a house. Although the house is in Hampstead, which even in the 19th-century was an affluent suburb, it is the back; it is not the public frontage of a grand house.

It is possible that this sketch was painted from one of the back windows of No. 2 Lower Terrace, Hampstead. Constable wanted to spend as much time with his family as possible and so made a makeshift studio in a small shed in the garden. It may be that this and the remarkable sketch *View in a Garden with a Red House Beyond* (*c.* 1821), with the washing line, were both done at this time.

A rainbow sweeps the sky from left to right, a motif seen in a sketch of Willy Lott's house and several other of Constable's compositions, both in sketches and major works. It is an effective device, which adds color and form to the sky while giving an extra dimension to the picture's overall compositional appeal.

RIVER LANDSCAPE (C. 1821–28)

Museo Lazaro Galdiano, Madrid. Courtesy of AKG

Photo

*I*N this wondrous, probably unfinished, painting, there is a seated figure on the grassy bank to the right under a vivid red umbrella, while to the left the path down to the cottages is suggested by stony sand-colored ground. Its inclusion within the work of the 1820s is based on subject-matter conjecture.

The scene is bathed in brilliant stormy evening light. The figure under the red umbrella attracts the eye, which in turn is drawn along the meandering river bank to the mid-ground of the painting and the ruin of a church. At a diagonal, opposite, and between the figure on the bank and the central ruin, is a small building with a spire, which may be St Nicholas' church, dedicated to fishermen.

In the foreground beneath the bank is a group of houses, that look like fisherman's cottages. Walking up a path to the right of the houses is a group of figures, possibly returning from work. Beyond the houses, towards the background of the composition, the land is waste-ground or perhaps simply unfinished. To the right of the painting, the scene appears to open out into the sea. The sky seems stormy and dark, flecked with bright blue on gray-white.

HAMPSTEAD: STORMY SUNSET (1822)

Courtesy of the V & A Picture Library

IT may be that Constable went to paint on Hampstead Heath in the early evening of the July 31, 1822. He commented that his eyes could rest once the sun had gone down and he would take advantage of the softer light to avoid straining them. In addition to the physical benefits, the evening light offered much to him in terms of *chiaroscuro*, the general atmosphere and the choice of colors he could legitimately use from his palette.

Harrow can be seen through the two small trees in the midground. The foreground retains a sense of light, the colors are those of the heath: burnt yellow, reds, and browns. There is a great deal of black and gray streaking across this area, with a single yellow stroke repeated almost directly above in the sky.

The sketch is hasty; it is dark and impending. The sky, partially worked up to show the tumult of the elements, presents a rainbow almost formed to the left.

STUDY OF CLOUDS (1822)

Courtesy of the V & A Picture Library

CONSTABLE inscribes this study of clouds, executed at noon on September 5, 1882: "Wind very brisk, and effect bright and fresh. Clouds moving very fast. With occasional very bright openings to the blue." In a letter dated 7 October, Constable tells his friend John Fisher, "I have made about fifty carefull [sic] studies of skies, tolerably large to be carefull."

There is no land at the bottom of this study as in, for instance, *Study of Sky and Trees* (*c.* 1821). Clearly, the sky is integral to Constable's landscapes and he found difficulty painting them more than once during his career, but believed: "The sky is the "source of light" in nature—and governs everything." The only other artist to have studied the sky in such detail and with such precision is Constable's contemporary, J. M. W. Turner, who undertook a similar "campaign of "skying'," but in watercolor rather than oil.

In this study, the paper is visible as a buff-colored ground against the white of the clouds, which shift ephemerally over the picture's surface. How to grab this moment, to show the transience of the sky against the static, familiar landscapes was a task that Constable undertook as a central and integral part of his entire work.

VIEW OF LOWER TERRACE, HAMPSTEAD (C. 1822)
Courtesy of the V & A Picture Library

*I*T is likely that this scene is Lower Terrace in Hampstead and therefore in perfect contrast to the "domestic" backyards of *The Grove* (*c.* 1821–22) and *View in a Garden with a Red House Beyond* (*c.* 1821). Here is a grander and more typical view of a middle-class house in Hampstead. The house is probably No. 4 Lower Terrace, although part of No. 3 can be seen on the right-hand side. Constable and his family rented No. 2 Lower Terrace for two summer seasons and it is known that he made a point of spending as much time with his family as possible while he was resident there. He painted what was at hand: the heath, the parish church, and trees and houses.

Painted with oil on canvas, this sketch may have been the final one for the finished painting intended for exhibition at the Royal Academy. This version is unfinished, with the tree on the left sketched in for position but with its foliage incomplete. This portion of the canvas was tucked in under the stretcher; this can be seen in the dark, smudged line that runs in a vertical line down the canvas.

STUDY OF CIRRUS CLOUDS (C. 1822)

Courtesy of the V & A Picture Library

THIS study of cirrus clouds may have been made as part of the series of "fifty carefull [sic] studies of skies" that Constable wrote to his friend John Fisher about, although the only one accurately dated and inscribed by the artist is *Study of Clouds* (1822).

It is possible that Constable had read meteorologist Luke Howard's (1771–1859) classification of cloud forms, describing cirrus as white, wispy clouds, as seen here skating across the paper. Painted on a sky-blue background, the clouds meet, dancing in daubs and strokes of cream-white, white, and gray. The paper shows through but is not used to any particular effect.

No sky study by Constable appears to have been directly transferred to another composition. This is not surprising, since what he was trying to achieve was an interpretation of the transience of the sky. The sky's formation is ever changing, quickly altering its color and reflected light. The studies show that Constable was simply "practising his scales", as it were, so that he could paint a sky effectively and interpret its ephemeral qualities accurately.

VIEW AT HAMPSTEAD, LOOKING DUE EAST (1823)
Courtesy of the V & A Picture Library

CONSTABLE was fond of painting in the evening, when the light had softened and the sky could be seen at its most dramatic. This oil sketch on paper depicts Hampstead Heath during the evening of August 26, 1823. The sky is darkening in an ominous way but, unusually for Constable, there are no descriptions on the back of the sketch about an approaching storm. The viewer looks up the path, on a level with the two figures walking along it. There are two figures on the right sitting on the grass.

This multi-directional composition, with its two sweeping contours leading the eye into the mid-ground with the two figures, two houses, and group of trees, is painted in a palette of greens, ranging from yellow-green to blue-green, gray and white. The path, which appears soft and sandy, is made up of various colors: burnt sienna, pink, and yellow, with some blue ground showing through.

The sky is a swirling mass of sweeps and strokes in gray, blue, white, and black with enough of the paper showing through to suggest the pink-yellow dying light of a summer's day.

266.8

A STONE IN THE GARDEN
OF COLEORTON HALL (1823)
Courtesy of the V & A Picture Library

DRAWN by Constable while visiting Sir George and Lady Beaumont, wealthy patrons of the arts, at Coleorton Hall in Leicestershire, this sketch shows the influence of Sir George (1753–1827), who was an accomplished dragftsman himself. Constable made copies after several of Beaumont's drawings during his six-week visit.

He also made copies after Claude during the same visit. In a letter to Maria, his wife, written on arrival at Coleorton, he says that he is writing "in a room full of Claudes ... real Claudes and Wilsons and Poussins, almost at the summit of my earthly ambitions."

Constable also made sketches in the grounds that he

The Close, Salisbury (1829)
Courtesy of the V & A Picture Library.
(See p. 202)

later used as a basis for his painting; for example, the drawing of *The Cenotaph to Joshua Reynolds,* exhibited at the Royal Academy in 1836. This drawing, in pencil and gray wash, shows a large rock in the foreground, surrounded by forest. The rock, largely in shadow, has cross-hatching on both sides and around its base, leaving a white highlight on the front edge. Beyond the rock stands a figure holding a stick. He may be reading a map. The wash, employed to denote foliage on the trees and ground, lends softness to the harsh pencil lines.

HELMINGHAM DELL, SUFFOLK
(C. 1823–26)
Musée du Louvre, Paris. Courtesy of AKG/Erich Lessing

*T*HIS oil sketch of Helmingham Dell closely resembles a finished painting of 1825–26, which was exhibited in 1833 and is now in Philadelphia. Constable began painting this subject in the early 1820s, although the composition for this painting is probably based on a drawing made about 20 years earlier when he was invited to stay by Lord Dysart, who owned Helmingham.

Two days after making the initial drawing, Constable wrote a letter to a friend saying: "Here I am quite alone among the oaks and solitude of Helmingham Park .... There are an abundance of trees of all sorts ...."

The viewer is situated among the trees looking up towards the bridge and over the watercourse. A small figure is sketched in, suggested by a red dash. The oak at the right of the composition gives the sketch a picturesque appeal. Constable noted that, although the scenery is not much, the place "affords good objects." "The Dell", as he called it, was serene, and just happened to be compositionally picturesque—an element that Constable used to his advantage.

SALISBURY CATHEDRAL FROM THE BISHOP'S GROUNDS (1823)
Courtesy of the V & A Picture Library

CONSTABLE'S friend, Archdeacon John Fisher, commissioned this painting for the Bishop of Salisbury. The painting was exhibited at the Royal Academy in 1823. A full-size copy and a small "wedding present" version exist, although Constable also made several views of the cathedral from various viewpoints.

One of the major issues surrounding this commission was the sky. Although at first the bishop accepted the painting with the dark cloud in the sky, a year later he asked Constable to "improve" it. A poignant comment follows by the bishop: "[If] Constable would but leave out his black clouds! Clouds are only black when it is going to rain. In fine weather the sky is blue."

Constable was working on his major painting *The Opening of Waterloo Bridge* (1817) for exhibition at the Royal Academy alongside this commission. To make matters more difficult, his entire family became ill, he had problems with his patron's framer and found the composition difficult, commenting: "It was the most difficult subject in landscape I ever had upon my easil [sic]."

The figures in the foreground of this painting are the bishop and his wife. The sky is blue but for the dark cloud to the left of the painting above the cathedral. The composition is picturesque and Classical, illustrating Claude and the old masters' influence on Constable's work.

THE CORNFIELD (1826)

The National Gallery, London. Courtesy of AKG Photo/Erich Lessing

*T*HIS is an example of Constable bowing to his rather conservative and unforgiving public. Here he painted a picture specifically to sell. It has all the "finish" that his work sometimes lacked. Further, it is in the popular and marketable picturesque style. The boy taking water, the dog, the sheep and the plough all have the rustic qualities that his buying public would have appreciated. Constable himself said of it, "it has certainly got a little more eye-salve than I usually condescend to give them."

Constable knew the countryside around Essex and Suffolk intimately, and he painted and studied it and understood its workings. The artist used motifs in this painting that he had sketched previously— the donkey, for instance, the boy drinking, and the dog. A similar dog appears in *The Haywain* (1821) and in the sketch and finished painting of *Hadleigh Castle* (1829).

As Constable's son, Charles Golding, pointed out, his father took some liberties with this scene: "The little church in the distance never existed; it is one of the rare instances where my father availed himself of the painter's licence to improve the composition."

The Cornfield is formulaic in this respect; it was made to please and, with luck, to sell. It was exhibited at the Royal Academy in 1826, went to the Salon de Paris in 1828 and was purchased by the artist's executors to be presented to the National Gallery, London, in 1837.

Full-size study for
***The Haywain* (c. 1821)**
Courtesy of the V & A Picture Library/K.F. Jackson. (See p. 138)

BRIGHTON BEACH (1824)

Courtesy of the V & A Picture Library

AN inscription by the artist on the back of this sketch reads: "Beach Brighton July 19. Noon. 1824. My Dear Minna's Birthday." "Minna" is Maria, Constable's wife. Despite his unflattering descriptions of Brighton, his output during this three-month stay in 1824 amounts to 12 oil sketches and several sketchbooks containing Brighton subjects. The family moved to Brighton in the hope that the sea air would cure Maria's ill-health.

This sketch shows a dark-golden beach, with a boulder revealed by the receding tide in the center of the horizontal plane. A fishing boat to the left of the rock is coming ashore, one of its crew already standing in the water and helping to haul the vessel on to the beach. More boats are following, presumably after a morning's fishing.

The sea is choppy; the surf is expressed in white highlights on the blue-gray and green. The tide follows the sweeping shore into the right-hand side of the painting. The sky, a gentle lilac-white with some blue, is brushed sketchily on to buff-colored paper that shows through the paint to create a fourth color. Some seagulls shoot down ready to meet the day's catch—part of the daily routine of Brighton beach.

BRIGHTON BEACH WITH
COLLIERS (1824)

Courtesy of the V & A Picture Library / K.F. Jackson

*T*HIS view of Brighton beach was painted on July 19, 1824, in the evening, looking eastwards; this we know from the notes Constable made on the back of the sketch. The artist and his family stayed in Brighton for the summer season and Constable spent three uninterrupted months there, during which time he produced a number of very beautiful sketches and drawings.

Compositionally, this is an interesting sketch. The beach and the sea claim approximately equal pictorial space that recedes from the foreground into the background. A horizontal line marks the horizon. Along the left-hand side are houses, beginning midway along the edge of the composition. The cliffs, bathed in the "very white and golden light" as described by Constable on the back of the sketch, stand out to form a clear continuation of the coastline and become the central axis of the composition.

Constable had a somewhat disparaging view of coastal scenes and sea painting. The clumsily sketched black collier (coal ship) obscuring the cliff may be a device to ensure that the picture was not a typical picturesque painting of the sea. Instead, he may have wanted to include the same "truth" and variety of motifs as in his more familiar landscape paintings.

BRIGHTON BEACH (1824)

Courtesy of the V & A Picture Library

ANOTHER sketch from the dozen or so painted at Brighton during Constable's first stay there on account of his wife Maria's bad health, this is extraordinarily animated, as he seldom included so many figures in his landscapes. He has inscribed the sketch: "Beach Brighton 22 July, 1824, very fine evening"

The evening light leaves long shadows on the beach. A boat appears in the central ground, nose up, pointing to the sky. A garish motif that resonates through the otherwise picturesque sketch, this may be another example of Constable's intolerance for seascape painting as a popular English genre.

The sand, sea, and sky converge just beyond the end of the boat and rock. Some sailing boats are placed, Armada-like, on the sea, their sails like feathers, painted delicately and lightly on to the sea's surface. A few more extend along the skyline.

Constable depicts adults and children out for an evening stroll, their garments still, suggesting that the wind is minimal, while their parasols protect them from the evening sun. They are little more than splashes of color, but Constable makes them seem wonderfully animated, suggesting that some are walking, while a couple on the right are chatting and two separate groups sit at the edge of the sea watching the sailing boats.

BRIGHTON BEACH (1824)
Courtesy of the V & A Picture Library

CONSTABLE was not enamoured of Brighton. Writing to his friend, Archdeacon John Fisher, he explains: "In short there is nothing here for a painter but the breakers—& sky—which have been lovely indeed and always varying." The Brighton sketches are largely concerned with the changing weather and ecstatic light, which is often more pronounced near the sea than inland.

This wide panoramic view depicts a July afternoon on Brighton beach, the gray sky broken on the right where the sun peers through the clouds on to the beach. It is about to rain. The beach is empty but

for two windblown figures. Their clothes, fluttering in the wind as they walk, are animated by the flick of a brush.

The composition, painted on a horizontal plain with sand in the foreground, sea in the mid-ground and the sky merging with the sea, comprises a palette of gray, white, and yellow. The black collier to the left of the figures interrupts the horizon. On the right, two tiny sketched boats float on the horizon, which is murky and unobtrusive.

The sand and sea, painted with long, smooth brushstrokes, contrast with the swirling strokes that Constable employed to paint the ever-changing sky.

BRIGHTON BEACH, WITH FISHING BOAT AND CREW (1824)
Courtesy of the V & A Picture Library

*T*HIS oil sketch, painted during Constable's trip to Brighton with his family, belongs in a series of about a dozen that he made and sent to his friend Archdeacon John Fisher for approval.

The sketch shows a shored-up fishing boat; the crew look as if they are sewing the sails, fixing the nets, and generally getting the boat ready for the next day's work. In and around the far side of the boat, members of the crew, sketched in black, white, and gray, are busily absorbed in their duties. A figure in the foreground, drawn with red hair, a yellow pullover, and blue trousers, stands in front of the boat. He may be varnishing or repairing the boat's woodwork and fixings.

The sea and the sky would merge together in their blue hue but for their opposing directional brushstrokes. The sky is painted with swift, upwards, slightly slanting, brushwork; the sea in vertical and very fine strokes. Only at the shore are the curling white breakers gently stroking the sand.

The light is beautiful; presumably it is evening since the crew would be out at sea in the early morning. Two sail ropes hang down, while one sail is unfurled, half of it in shadow. A bundle of nets lie in the foreground to the right.

A WINDMILL NEAR BRIGHTON (1824)
Courtesy of the V & A Picture Library

*I*NTERESTINGLY, this oil sketch is inscribed on the back as follows: "Brighton August, 3 1824 Smock or Tower Mill west end of Brighton—consists of London cow fields—and hideous masses of unfledged earth called the country."

Painted in oil on paper, the sketch shows a glorious scene over the South Downs with Tower Mill on the right. In the foreground cattle are grazing on dry, yellow-brown earth with just a hint of green. Beyond, to the left, the Downs splay out into a hilly patchwork which drops off in the center to become blue haze reminiscent of *View at Hampstead, Looking Towards London*, (1833). There is very little green on the landscape but heavy use of brown, yellow, black, and gray. The sky is pink, blue, and gray, moving swiftly and leaving a dark shadow as it passes.

Though the general coloration of this painting is muted, the sky is dramatic and visually very exciting. The windmill allows the overall composition a subject, and this is evidently the gripe here: the artist cannot find the visual stimulus in the landscape that he is accustomed to painting in his native Suffolk.

HOVE BEACH (1824)
Courtesy of the V & A Picture Library

THIS view in Hove, Sussex, not far from Brighton, projects a romantic vision of the sea as dynamic and mysterious, overpowering, and beautiful. The sea takes up two-thirds of the foreground and mid-ground, while the sky fills half of the canvas horizontally. The sand borrows a small corner on the left and the tide rushes in, the waves fast and furious against the shore. A solitary figure walks on the beach, which slopes down towards the sea.

The sky is stormy: a large, gray cloud showers rain on the scene. The sea is green-blue with crests of white, which come to a crescendo on the shore and throw up yellow sand—just suggested by two short paint strokes on the breakers. Several sails are dotted about on the horizon, while a sketchy boat is coming into view just off-center on the skyline.

Evidence of some *pentimenti,* or "painting out", is visible with the naked eye on the skyline, left by Constable's alterations to the positions of the sailing boats. The figure and the indecisively painted boat are positioned diagonally opposite each other.

A WINDMILL AMONG HOUSES, WITH A RAINBOW (C. 1824)

Courtesy of the V & A Picture Library

*T*HE windmill is a recurring motif in Constable's work, as is the rainbow, normally abstracted from the real landscape and exploited because he liked the way they looked in the composition. He saw his role very much as someone who could see elements in nature that others could not: a sort of visionary who imposed his view on the world.

This oil sketch may show the same windmill in *A Windmill Near Brighton* (1824). The current sketch is not inscribed by the artist, and so it is impossible to verify where it belongs in Constable's *oeuvre* except by visual similarities with other work of the period.

The rainbow, painted pink, white, and blue, falls from a pink cloud and lands just behind the windmill. The paddles pick up the light forming the rainbow opposite, the right-hand paddle pasted with thick impasto-white, while the other half is black. The vertical paddle is yellow-gray at the top and gray with a hint of yellow at the bottom. They appear static, suggesting that there is no wind.

STUDY FOR
THE LEAPING HORSE (C. 1825)
Courtesy of the V & A Picture Library

FOLLOWING his return to London from Brighton in 1824, Constable began work on *The Leaping Horse* (1824–25), which he intended would be one of his large canvases based on themes of the river and canal. This sketch is full size.

The palette is dark—brown, brown-gray, some yellow, greens, green-gray, and flecks of white. In the sky, blue, blue-gray, and white contrast with the leaves and branches of the tree, which begins another muted harmony of yellow-brown against blue-gray.

The horse rears, with the boy behind it looking over the edge of the bridge. The red harness on the horse and the red in the boy's jacket add color, but the intensely dark palette of the overall composition makes even this appear muted. The willow stump on the right creates an arc through which the horse leaps, although the most central compositional motif is the drinking cow, which has disappeared in the final work.

In the mid-ground two boats pass; the people on them appear oblivious to the barge horse rearing, which indicates that this was a very familiar occurrence. In the foreground, the water rushing through the floodgates and the old bridge with knotted flora and fauna entangled in it, express the naturalness, permanence and age-old tradition of barge horses that worked on the river Stour.

AN OAK IN DEDHAM MEADOWS (1827)
Courtesy of the V & A Picture Library

*T*HIS pencil and watercolor drawing was sketched on October 6, 1827 while Constable was on holiday with his two eldest children in the neighborhood of Flatford in Suffolk. He had not been back to the area for a holiday since his last visit with Maria, his wife, in 1817.

The oak butts up against the foreground in a serpentine twist. Some cross-hatching in pencil around the lower trunk casts a shadow around the base of the tree, helping it to appear grounded and placed firmly within the landscape. It is an enduring image, for although the tree looks dead, it is wonderfully animated. The leafless, sinewy branches reach out to both sides of the paper, filling the top part of the picture and receding into the background. The sky is completely flat and only the branches of the tree decorate the upper part of the picture. The landscape appears flat and dwarfed by the enormous oak in the foreground.

The tree has the look of a dripping candle. Painted in varying shades of brown, with some red-and-black pencil marks still visible beneath the watercolor, the surface is knarled. The lower branches have been broken off and their dry and rotten appearance is clearly evoked. The trees in the background on the right are green and leafy, in contrast to the oak, which looks so very bare and stark in its autumnal nakedness.

A Watermill at Gillingham, Dorset (c. 1827)

Courtesy of the V & A Picture Library

*T*HERE are three paintings depicting Gillingham watermill or, as it was known, Parham's or Perne's mill. All three are similar, although this painting is the only portrait version of the subject and the only one to have the two men grinding their scythes, seen on the left of the composition.

This painting may have been a commission from John Perne Tinney, who had a family connection with the mill and whom Constable referred to when writing to his friend, Archdeacon John Fisher in Salisbury: "Tinney ... is anxious to have his ancestors' mill, and a view of Salisbury ...."

The gable-end of the mill house stands central to the composition at an imposing but slightly oblique angle. The mill wheel chugs round, visibly forcing water back into the millstream and beautifully rendered by Constable in a rush of frothy white paint, which hits the otherwise murky green-gray of the water. The scene is industrious. Four men can be seen doing their work about the place. The mill itself looks well-worn and slightly tired. The bank on the left-hand side of the picture holds a foreground of plants and wild flowers that hang over into the water, and trees then rise upwards to the mauve-gray, white, and blue sky.

***A Windmill Near Brighton* (c. 1828)**
Courtesy of the V & A Picture Library. (See p. 194)

BRANCH HILL POND, HAMPSTEAD (1828)
Courtesy of the V & A Picture Library

*O*F all the pictures depicting Branch Hill Pond in Hampstead, this is the one that most resembles the initial sketch of 1819. Many of the motifs already in the sketch are worked to a finished composition here. It is a matter of taste whether the viewer finds Constable's working towards a final painting more visually exciting than the finished product.

He was continually criticized for producing work that appeared unfinished. It was therefore imperative that, as a serious painter with a wife and family to support, a substantial portion of Constable's work attracted people with the financial (and probably social) means to buy it.

That said, this work of 1828 has resolved this problem in that he seems to have come to grips with a composition that is pleasing to the eye. The familiar horse and cart, a motif that Constable knew would attract a buyer, is fully rendered. The vista, open and not hampered by cloud, is very pleasant, almost idyllic. The general atmosphere of the scene and its conventional rendering gave it a good chance of being sold at the Royal Academy when it was exhibited in 1828 or 1830, under the title *Landscape*.

COAST SCENE AT BRIGHTON: EVENING (1828)

Courtesy of the V & A Picture Library

*T*HIS view may be of Chalybeate Wells, Brighton, which was a popular walk. The evening sunset composition shows several groups and individual figures out for an evening walk. They all seem to take the same course, with some people on the left just beginning their walk, and others disappearing into the right mid-ground, walking into the sunset. Their hastily drawn shapes are masterful flicks of the brush in black, blue, white, red, and pink.

The sky takes up two-thirds of the picture space. The sun glowing in the center of the painting is an off-white splash, surrounded by yellow against orange. Some blue is still visible on the left, which melts into mauve-pink, butting against the huge black cloud which moves to the right. Some streaks of pure orange pigment occasionally sweep the sky.

The landscape fits gently against the violent colors of the sky, the undulating skyline softening the blow as the earth hits the fiery sky. On the left, there appears to be a chalkpit, or perhaps sand. In the mid-ground, a field hugs some stumps where trees once stood.

COAST SCENE WITH VESSELS AT BRIGHTON (1828)
Courtesy of the V & A Picture Library

*T*HIS pencil and gray wash sketch, made on May 30, 1828, shows Constable at his finest as a draftsman and observer. The sketch, inscribed in the top left-hand corner by the artist, records a sequence of events he witnessed over a period of 48 hours.

Constable was in Brighton once more because of his wife Maria's ill health. He spent much of his time sketching around the beach, but must have come to draw this event as a reporter, drawing swiftly as the action unfurled.

The schooner *Malta* was beached at Brighton after a raging storm that began on May 28. Here it is seen with another boat aground in the near distance. Constable took particular interest in the fate of *Malta* and made five, possibly six, drawings of the events of the day. Here, we witness the activity around the ship as she is levered out of the sand by a group of men using heavy poles. The foreground is crowded with activity that is totally focused on the grounded boat. *Malta* slants to the center of the composition, the stricken boat unsteady on her hull and uneasy out of the water.

A WINDMILL NEAR BRIGHTON (C. 1828)

Courtesy of the V & A Picture Library

*T*HIS restless sketch of a windmill, drawn showing the mill rather than its decorative paddles, is unusual in Constable's work. It was engraved in mezzotint by the artist's friend and colleague, David Lucas, for inclusion in an edition of *English Landscape Scenery* which was published in the 1830s.

The sketch is inspired and dramatic: the palette is impressionistic and brutal. Worked with a palette knife, the paint was laid on rapidly. The sketch is a wondrously inventive scene, "mystified" by placing a windmill within a landscape in Brighton that should be recognizable but is not.

The windmill is the only clearly defined motif in the sketch. One of its paddles, brown-orange in the light, places a dark, diagonal line of shadow across the otherwise white mill. There are several

openings, into which a line of smoke from one of the chimneys appears. On the right, a multi-colored wall, tree or bush obstructs part of our view of the landscape. In the foreground on the right, a patch of yellow may suggest a field that butts on to a millhouse, whose chimneys emit smoke. A figure in gray is just discernible entering the door of the mill from under the porch.

Detail from *A Watermill at Gillingham, Dorset* (c. 1827)
Courtesy of the V & A Picture Library. (See p. 186)

SKETCH FOR HADLEIGH CASTLE (C. 1828–29)

The Tate Gallery, London. Courtesy of AKG/Erich Lessing

CONSTABLE visited Hadleigh Castle, Kent once in 1814. While he was there, he made a pencil sketch which, 15 years later, he was to refer to for a major painting exhibited at the Royal Academy in 1829.

In many ways, the oil study for Hadleigh Castle is more breathtaking than the finished work. The brush strokes are looser, the sky more dramatic and intense. It has a sense of nature's dynamics—all its sudden violent changes and its ability to make humanity feel vulnerable and small.

What is notable in the *Hadleigh Castle* sketch are the steps toward Romanticism: that is, Constable's concern not with the particular—the flora and fauna, the workings of barges, mills or rural life, but with the universal—man's unease with nature and the violent and unpredictable behavior of the elements.

Constable's wife Maria died in November 1828, leaving him, he said, with a void in his heart "that can never be filled again in this world." The restlessness of the imagery, a ruin surrounded by sea and sky that is so unbearably desolate and uncontained, could well reflect his grief of mind. Several paintings of similarly desolate subjects are produced after this date, notably *Stonehenge* (1836), and *Old Sarum* (1834).

A View at Salisbury from Archdeacon Fisher's House (1829)

Courtesy of the V & A Picture Library

CONSTABLE apparently painted this view from one of the windows in the south wing of Archdeacon John Fisher's house in Cathedral Close at Salisbury. There are three such studies, all of which were probably painted from the windows at the close during the two visits he made in July and November 1829.

The foreground is seen from directly below the window. Part of a wall at an oblique angle enters the picture plane, meeting another wall around the garden and paddock. A knee-high metal fence encloses the flower garden, which is probably the private garden of the Fisher's residence. Beyond that is a walled garden, which is busy with bushes and shrubs, small flowerbeds, and decorative paths. Past the wall a horse is grazing in the meadow among the long shadows created by the trees.

The tree to the left is half in the composition, and, like the oblique and horizontal walls, is presented only partially, giving the scene an overall boundary around its right edge.

The eye is attracted away from this axis to the horse and then follows this diagonally through the trees across the picture. Harnham Ridge can be glimpsed in the distance.

The Close, Salisbury (1829)
Coutesy of the V & A Picture Library. (See p. 202)

SALISBURY CATHEDRAL FROM THE MEADOWS (C. 1829)

Courtesy of Christie's Images

THIS oil sketch of *Salisbury Cathedral from the Meadows* probably dates from 1829, earlier than the painting of the same name that was exhibited at the Royal Academy in 1831. This study, although a view towards the cathedral from the meadows, is quite different in style and composition.

The palette is glaringly gray-white. On the left of the picture, there is a patch of bright red. Is it a jacket or a bicycle? It is difficult to make out. The foliage in the foreground and the trees framing the picture on the right are autumnal: yellow-brown and burnt orange. The colors are warm and rich until the mid-ground center, when the light seems to saturate the view. The sky is formed by strokes of the palette knife in blue-gray and white. The surface shows through, giving the sky texture, the roughness of which suits the restless nature of this view.

None of the glorious light, peaceful atmosphere or compositional cliché of *Salisbury Cathedral from the Meadows* (1831) is evident here. However, the sketch resembles a drawing made around the same time: *Salisbury Cathedral from the North-West* (c. 1829). Similarly, it resembles a mezzotint by David Lucas of Salisbury published after Constable's death in *English Landscape Scenery*, (1838).

THE CLOSE, SALISBURY (1829)

Courtesy of the V & A Picture Library

*A*N inscription on the back of this sketch reads: "Close—15 July—1829 11 o'clock noon—Wind S.W—very fine." A succinct description that may help us look at the sketch and appreciate the painting more than we otherwise would do?

In this close-up study, virtually none of the lawn in the grounds at Salisbury is visible but for a small shadowed segment on the right of the picture with a lake beyond it. Some splashes of color, which may be Constable's signatures for some figures, are visible among the trees. On the far right, next to the lake, some strokes of red, yellow, and white look like ornaments hanging in the branches of the tree.

The view homes in on the left, with the trees receding into the background. The dry, sand-colored landscape, seen briefly on the left behind the trees and sketchily on the right, slopes down across the picture from left to right. The wind blows south-westerly, bending the trees slightly and rustling their leaves. The cloud, blown briskly across the sky and suspended above the trees, creates a contrast of yellow-green and dark-green against the white, blue, and pink of the sky.

A VIEW AT SALISBURY, FROM THE LIBRARY OF ARCHDEACON FISHER'S HOUSE (1829)

Courtesy of the V & A Picture Library

THIS sketch incorporates the same group of trees as in *The Close, Salisbury* (1829), but from a more distant view and in the mid-afternoon light. The pictures were painted in the same month and year.

Here, the group of trees shown in *The Close, Salisbury* is positioned on the far left. The figures suggested in that view are now one figure, which is slightly more defined and apparently sitting on a bench facing the sun-lit lake. Behind the bench a path arches round and leads from the bottom left-hand corner of the composition down to the lake, getting increasingly thinner until it becomes a fine red line.

A large and ominous gray cloud sinks behind the trees, while to the right the sky is a lovely midsummer's-evening hue of pink and blue with the odd gray cloud beginning to form. The sun is casting long shadows, which begins a train of shadow moving around to the figure on the bench. The landscape slopes down to the right beyond the trees, elevates slightly and then fans out into the distance. Two tall conifers stand erect but tiny on the last piece of gray land before we exit the picture on the right.

STUDY OF CLOUDS ABOVE A WIDE LANDSCAPE (1830)
Courtesy of the V & A Picture Library

*T*HIS study of clouds, inscribed by the artist: "About 11—noon—Sept 15 1830. Wind—W", is made in pencil and watercolor. The view is of Hampstead, painted from the window of the house Constable and his family rented during the summer of 1830, No. 6 Well Walk. Constable enthused about the view from the drawing room: " ... our little drawing room commands a view unequalled in Europe ... The dome of St Paul's in the air, realizes Michelangelo's idea on seeing that of the Pantheon—'I will build such a thing in the sky.'"

There is very little of the landscape to see, although its very smallness is of great effect in allowing the sky to take over the painting, surfing over the scene and generating a feeling of the breadth and ever-changing movement over the landscape. The large gray cloud at the top of the study looms over the scene as if in motion. This work uses a similar blue-gray palette to that used in *View of Hampstead Looking Towards London* (1833), showing the dome of St Paul's.

STOKE-BY-NAYLAND, SUFFOLK (C. 1830)

Courtesy of the V & A Picture Library

*D*AVID LUCAS worked in collaboration with Constable, adapting this oil
sketch for inclusion in the mezzotints
in the edition of *English Landscape Scenery* of
December 1830. The composition was
probably taken from a number of sketches
made some time earlier and the final work
painted in the artist's studio.

The sketch altered dramatically once
published in *English Landscape Scenery,* although
the church remained. In the mezzotint, the
trees on the right-hand side pull back to reveal
a magnificent rainbow and a flock of birds.
The rainbow becomes the central focus for the
entire composition.

Here, the light falls on the woman
carrying her bundle. The ground is red, overlaid
with brown and white. The woman's posture is
contrapposto, that is, with her weight shifted to
one side, giving her a slightly twisted, although
elegant, stance.

The trees on the right present a
darkened avenue through which the woman
will pass. Tracks are visible on the ground,
drawn in with extraordinarily deliberate marks
scratched into the paint ground. The tracks
lead diagonally from foreground to mid-
ground. The sky is hastily sketched in, white
around the church moves across to blue behind
the trees. The church and the group of buildings
around it close off the horizon, forcing the eye
back into the foreground light.

STOKE-BY-NAYLAND, SUFFOLK (C. 1830)

Courtesy of the V & A Picture Library

*T*HE publication of some designs drawn by Constable in mezzotint for *English Landscape Scenery* in 1830 may have offered the incentive to create this monochrome sketch and two other similar sepia wash drawings.

The sketch bears comparison with the oil sketch *Stoke-by-Nayland, Suffolk (c.* 1830), although it has more in common with the finished mezzotint. It may be that Constable intended to generalize the scene so that it could be any church in any English village, although he borrowed compositional elements from previous sketches.

The lights and darks created by the sepia on white paper are employed to contrast the white of the church against the dark hill and the light of what is possibly moonlight accenting the curve of the hilltop. The moonlight reflects on the white stone of the church and places a pool of light on the right–hand edge towards the foreground. Further back a tree is in darkness, then another pool of light appears and disappears behind the church, backlighting part of the tree on the right. On the left, the houses and a portion of the slope in the foreground are highlighted, the light ricocheting from one side of the composition to the other.

A COUNTRY ROAD WITH TREES AND FIGURES (C. 1830)

Courtesy of the V & A Picture Library

*T*HIS sketch in oil on canvas is drawn from the same spot as *A Cart on the Lane to Flatford* (1811). Stylistically, in the technique it could possibly be placed in the same period as that painting.

The view is certainly the same, although this time a man on a mule in a red jacket is coming down the lane into the foreground. The same tree is on the right and the bend is still obscured by hedgerows, trees, and bushes. On the left, the layby graduates up to the field behind the hedge. This time a gate into the field is drawn in white. Two figures, a man sitting and a woman standing, are either waiting or resting on the grassy bank. Beyond them the landscape opens into a fertile vista of fields, trees, and houses.

The use of color in this sketch compared to the palette of 1811 is tame. Here, the color of the trees and bushes on the right is several shades of brown, yellow, black, and green. On the left, the color is a muted harmony of browns and greens with some gray on the horizon. The sky is hastily painted in criss-crossing strokes of blue, white, and gray.

A COUNTRY ROAD
AND SANDBANK (*C.* 1830–36)
Courtesy of the V & A Picture Library

*I*N this late oil sketch Constable poses a remarkable challenge to the conventions of color and tone, perspective and spatial planes, subject, and composition. The viewer enters the picture along a mustard-brown path that only just covers the brown ground underneath. The path sweeps round to the right, its bend highlighted with a splash of white. Only such erratic brushwork and color as this could make such a non-subject interesting. The thick paint, brushed on in sweeps and dashes, is in a startling palette of earth and warmer red tones that allow the texture of the paper underneath to show through the paint.

The sky is a wondrous mix of white-yellow, gray, brown, blue, pink, and lilac. A dark blue patch of land meets the sky just between the two trees. One tree leans down from the left-hand bank, while opposite on the right is the sandbank, the top of which is brown. The side of the sandbank facing the path reflects the pink light visible in streaks through the sky; the colors then helter-skelter down the sandbank, swirling in brown, gray, and yellow-white.

VIEW OF THE STOUR:
DEDHAM CHURCH IN THE DISTANCE (C. 1832–36)
Courtesy of the V & A Picture Library

*T*HIS late pen and sepia sketch is a dazzling studio-based study of an earlier work, *Dedham Lock and Mill* (1819). Taking the central section of the church, Constable explores one of his most enduring concerns as a painter of nature: how to reflect the wonders of nature's light. Here, this exploration is brought to its final compelling conclusion.

The artist's preoccupation with *chiaroscuro* is evident in the dark sepia ink against the whiteness of the paper. This daring abstraction denies color in describing the place, its shifting light and general mood. Instead, the monochrome drawing is a statement of Constable's belief in the "chiaroscuro of nature" in its most dramatic and confident form. It is likely that Constable's collaboration with his friend and colleague David Lucas in preparing mezzotints for publication in *English Landscape Scenery*, first published in 1830, prompted Constable's need to consolidate his thoughts about *chiaroscuro*.

Dedham Church, represented here from a slightly different viewpoint, is now closer to the tree on the right. The water in the foreground, the bridge over the sluice and the tree are recognizable elements of a familiar scene. There is no need for detail in this exercise, only attention to the light and shade of the scene.

Dedham Lock and Mill (1820)
Courtesy of AKG Photo. (See p. 108)

A BARGE ON THE STOUR (C. 1832)

Courtesy of the V & A Picture Library

MADE in pencil, pen, ink, and watercolor this is a variation on the theme seen in many of Constable's works. The drawing is from a page in a sketchbook and it is thought that the watercolor was made on a visit to East Bergholt in 1832.

The barge in the left foreground, with the young peasant girl sitting down while the standing boatman rows her down the river, appears in at least two other sketches. The white horse in the foreground apparently stands solidly and still in the water while its rider dismounts. The river continues up through the composition, under the tree and away to the left.

The boatman and girl resemble the pair from *The Valley Farm* (1835), and *A Farmhouse Near the Water's Edge* (c. 1835). The horse might be, for its inattentive and obedient stillness, a copy of the brown horse in *Flatford Mill* (1816–17).

Because Constable continually reworked views and reused motifs, constantly sketching, noting, and reconsidering compositions, either in nature or from sketches, we can recognize motifs in his paintings with ease.

TREES AND STRETCH OF WATER
ON THE STOUR (C. 1832–36)
Courtesy of the V & A Picture Library

*T*HIS sketch, like the one that precedes it, is a studio drawing of an earlier composition— *A Barge on the Stour* (*c.* 1832), which was drawn from nature. Here, the artist abstracts the central section of the picture to show the boy and the front of the barge, the water and the background trees.

The desired *chiaroscuro* effect is achieved by employing the white of the paper to contrast with the brown ink, painted in relaxed, heavy strokes and repainted on top of dry ink in places to achieve a darker, denser brown. The tree on the right bends into the picture to enclose the scene. The heavy barge enters from the right, the oarsman now outside the picture. It floats horizontally through the picture, just in front of or behind the boy and the horse. The shape of the boy clambering on to his horse is still distinguishable, the back of the horse white against the heavily drawn-in dark brown bow of the boat.

The medium expresses the water extending into the background of the composition. The strokes of splendid wash leave shapes of white like light reflected on water.

A Barge on the Stour (*c.* 1832)
Courtesy of the V & A Picture Library. (See p. 218)

ENGLEFIELD HOUSE, BERKSHIRE (1833)
Courtesy of the V & A Picture Library

*T*HIS watercolor sketch is a study for a painting exhibited at the Royal Academy in 1833, with the title *Englefield House, Berkshire, the Seat of Richard Benyon-de Bouvoir, Esq.—Morning.* The title for the finished painting is significant as it seems that the Academy suggested that Constable's picture should hang in the "Architectural Room", as it was "only" a picture of a house. Constable maintained that it was "a picture of a summer morning, including a house."

It is not clear why, this late in his career, and without needing to for financial reasons, Constable is painting portraits of country estates when, as he said himself: "a gentleman's park—is my aversion." There are several versions of this study, drawn on Constable's visit to Englefield in August 1832, accompanied by his friend and sponsor Samuel Lane.

The view in the sketch resembles the finished painting quite closely. However, it seems that Constable may have misinterpreted his patron's wishes. First, Benyon-de Bouvoir did not like the cows in the foreground, which Constable replaced with deer, then, as Lane related, he did not like the "specky or spotty appearance of your touch." If Constable had stuck to this study, it seems likely that his client would have more graciously received the finished painting.

A COTTAGE IN A CORNFIELD (1833)

Courtesy of the V & A Picture Library

*P*ROBABLY exhibited by Constable at the Royal Academy in 1833 and at the British Institution in 1834, this painting may have been lying around for some time before Constable decided to show it, as he commented in a letter of 1833: "I have brushed up my Cottage into a pretty look …."

The cottage stands alone, surrounded by a field of ripening corn. One of Constable's biographers commented: "The cottage in this little picture is closely surrounded by corn, which on the side most shaded from the sun remains green, while over the rest of the field it has ripened; one of many circumstances that may be discovered in Constable's landscapes, which mark them as the productions of an incessant observer of nature."

The donkey on the left has its precedent in an earlier sketch. It stands motionless by the fence with a dash of red across its head. The dried mud, grass, and flowers in the foreground are painted in jewel-like detail. The branches of the tree on the right-hand side of the picture sweep the sky, which is abundant with a growing number of stacked cumulus clouds.

Willy Lott's House with a Rainbow (c. 1820)
Courtesy of Christie's Images. (See p. 110)

VIEW AT HAMPSTEAD LOOKING TOWARDS LONDON (1833)

Courtesy of the V & A Picture Library

PAINTED on 7 December, 1833, this winter scene of Hampstead looking towards St Paul's Cathedral belongs with a series of five watercolors of the same subject painted between June 1831 and December 1833. The painting, executed from a back window of his house in Well Walk, Hampstead, shows a darkening winter palette of three colors: green, blue-gray and brown. The paper, which shows through, is used to offset the brown, giving the *chiaroscuro* effect that Constable worked so hard achieve.

The scene shows the huge dome of St Paul's looming mistily and slightly off-center as the focus of the composition. The scene is built up horizontally across the paper; but it can be read as radiating outwards from the dome, creating an extraordinary panoramic affect. This illusion is created partly by the sky, painted in broad, sweeping brush strokes, that radiate towards the edges of the paper. The medium is used to maximum advantage to create a rainy, misty hue—a wet and stormy afternoon that will pass, which is so very evocative of the time of year. Constable noted it as December, "3 o'clock—very stormy afternoon—and high wind."

Constable used watercolors frequently during his later career and his use of the medium became increasingly confident and free.

STOKE POGES CHURCH, BUCKINGHAMSHIRE (ILLUSTRATION TO GRAY'S *ELEGY*) (1833)
Courtesy of the V & A Picture Library

*T*HIS preparatory watercolor was designed for an engraving to illustrate Thomas Gray's (1716–1771) *Elegy Written in a Countryside Churchyard*, and was to be published by Constable's friend John Martin (1789–1854) in 1834. This particular sketch, however, was never published as an engraving.

It is doubtful that the watercolor was drawn from nature, although it is possible that Constable may have used an engraving or drawing by someone else for guidance. This seems unlikely, however, and a more plausible suggestion is that Constable delved into a sketchbook going back some 20 years and found a sketch that would suffice. The sketchbook of 1813 acts as a journal of Constable's early career and is an important source of reference, especially for his later work, when a greater portion of his time was spent in his studio working from drawings and sketches made earlier in the open air.

Stoke Poges church sits on the top of a hill surrounded by trees; a transitory flock of birds flies above it. The graveyard is fenced off to the right and runs down from the church, where the scene is bright and light. The foreground, in contrast, lies in dark shadow. On the left, a group of trees reach up into the mauve-and-white sky.

STUDY FOR A LANDSCAPE (*C.* 1833–36)
Courtesy of the V & A Picture Library

*P*AINTED at the end of Constable's career, this watercolor is a beautifully loose, positive view of what may be a Suffolk scene drawn from nature during a visit in 1833. The composition bears a generic resemblance to that of *The Cornfield* (1826).

Although Constable wrote that on a trip with Charles Golding Constable, his son, in 1833, Golding worked and he "did nothing", it is possible that the drawing was made from nature. Possibly, however, like the monochrome drawings of this period, it may have been drawn from sketches made earlier.

In the watercolor the colors are bright, airy, and loosely painted. The palette is a soft, yet strong mix of yellow, green, brown, pink wash, mauve, and blue. The landscape is very open; the lights, provided by the white of the paper, are very bright. There are clouds in the sky but they are not ominous as Constable's clouds sometimes could be. Shadow bathes the left-hand side of the canvas beneath the trees, and a shadow of the tree in the mid-ground lies across the path, purely for atmosphere and effect. The overall tone of the scene remains radiant.

Full-size study for *The Haywain* (**c. 1821**)
Courtesy of the V & A Picture Library/K.F. Jackson. (See p. 138)

HAMPSTEAD HEATH FROM NEAR WELL WALK (1834)
Courtesy of the V & A Picture Library

*P*AINTED on April 12, 1834, this watercolor is a breathtakingly vivid representation of the landscape around Hampstead Heath. The artist notes on the back of the paper: "Spring Clouds—hail Squalls ...." Considering that Constable was, for most of his career, a very conservative painter who believed that he should represent the "truth" in nature, this interpretation of the heath in spring is especially surprising. It prompts the question: did the artist see the heath like this on this particular day? Were the colors this vivid and in such perfect, glaring contrast?

This picture may also prompt us to consider the idea of representation itself. It may provoke in us, the viewer, some sense of ease because, after all, "seeing" is as subjective as representation itself. To the modern eye, it is not so surprising to see a watercolor of such unconventional vivacity and tonal disharmony.

MIDDLETON CHURCH (1835)

Courtesy of the V & A Picture Library

*T*AKEN from a sketchbook of 50 pages, this drawing shows Middleton Church in Sussex. Constable made four drawings of the church, one showing a delicately drawn skeleton revealed by erosion in the graveyard. This sketch illustrates the church and records the erosion. Charlotte Smith (1748–1806) in "Sonnet written in the Church-yard of Middleton", likewise recalls:

"The sea no more its swelling surf confines,
But o'er the shrinking land sublimely rides!"

The land, eaten away by erosion, shows red-brown against the soft green of the grass. In one section of the strata, a white-gray highlight marks a line of time in the earth. The church teeters precariously on the edge of a desolate, wet and marshy looking beach. In the church-yard are what appear to be three figures.

The sky is a sepulchral mauve, echoing the sky in *Stonehenge* (1836) and an earlier watercolor made in Hampstead that has an equally glorious sky contrasted with a yellow landscape *Hampstead Heath from near Well Walk* (1834). The brown roof of the church is in harmonious contrast with the mauve-pink tones of the sky. The church, which stands perpendicular to the picture plane, has a series of blind arches, which stand out as shadows against the stone surface.

VIEW IN THE GROUNDS OF ARUNDEL CASTLE (1835)

Courtesy of the V & A Picture Library

MADE while Constable was on a visit to Arundel with his two eldest children, this dark and imposing pencil and watercolor sketch is found in a sketchbook that includes several other drawings and watercolors made at the castle and in the surrounding woodland. The beauty of the castle struck Constable to such a degree that he felt its influence immediately, saying, " ... for I have too much preferred the picturesque to the beautiful—which I hope will account for the broken ruggedness of my style."

The watercolor shows a dramatic scene, looking up to the castle from the ground. The castle looms above the trees; silver birches march up the side of the rugged, mountainous slope of the hill, their willowy trunks painted translucent silver-white. On the ground is a tower with a bridge. A dark tunnel enters the hillside. Light brushes the façade of the tower, its ghostly fingers stroking it in streaks of seal-color wash. The palette is dark brown and green, with some yellow and paler green as highlights. The sky is darkening into evening in a wash of mauve, pink, and white.

DEDHAM MILL (C. 1835)
Courtesy of Christie's Images

THIS view of Dedham Mill is a late study, for which some improvisation is evident. Constable does not get much more impressionistic than this, and calls to mind Claude Monet's (1840–1926) later work of water lilies.

This is an astounding painting. The mill, to the left of the painting and almost hidden by trees, stands obliquely to the picture plane. The waterwheel, distinguishable against the mill, has its movement suggested by flecks of white. A boat just beneath this in the water bobs around, the water disturbed by the wheel plunging into the reservoir.

The palette is an incredibly rich variety of red-browns, blue, ochre-yellow, pink, white, bright red, and green. The paint is all but daubed, almost splashed on to create a scene—an atmosphere—which can be recognized but which is nonetheless a daringly impressionistic rendition of a place that Constable could have painted in minute, naturalistic detail.

This departure into improvisation characterizes the later work of Constable; it is necessary to compare this scene with earlier works in order to establish the painting's subject and location. Compare this to the sketch for *Dedham Mill* (*c.* 1810–15), or consider *The Opening of Waterloo Bridge* (1832), which is more jewel-like in its brisk brushwork but is similarly invigorated by Constable's colors and brushwork.

SKETCH FOR THE VALLEY FARM (C. 1835)
Courtesy of the V & A Picture Library

THIS compositional sketch in oil possibly antedates the final picture by ten years or so. Constable exhibited the finished painting at the Royal Academy in 1835. The motif of the oarsman in his boat replaces that of the child seen sitting down rowing the boat in an earlier sketch for the painting. In the final painting, the oarsman and the girl are both in the boat, which has moved further upstream to the right of the tree.

Only the roof of Willy Lott's Suffolk house catches the sunlight, while the remainder of the building is in dark shadow. This feature remains a constant throughout the series, although the final angle is shifted and the house is more visually central to the composition. In front of the house is clear space, depicting a path with a boat and a figure. Previously, this area was a V-shaped white-yellow line and still unresolved.

The sky in this sketch is blue and darker than in the previous version. The voluminous dark green tree does not help what is already a very enclosed and dark composition. Constable repairs this in the final painting, lightening the sky with some white cloud and opening out the right-hand side with a less leafy, sculptural tree.

A Mill on the Banks of the River Stour (1802)
Courtesy of the V & A Picture Library. (See p. 32)

A River Scene, with a Farmhouse
Near the Water's Edge (c. 1835)

Courtesy of the V & A Picture Library

CONSTABLE'S later oil sketches are unhesitatingly strong and confident. It may be that these studio sketches can be viewed as reminiscences, using sketches made from nature many years beforehand in his beloved Suffolk. While this may be so, the artist appears to have made an absolute breakthrough in his technique, in his vigorous handling of paint and his new energy for cherished places. His observations seem to lead him somewhere quite new: nature is there, the light and the movement, the colors, and the textures, but they are translated and communicated to the viewer in a new and fresh way.

The art-loving public of the early 19th century were seeing a glimpse of what was to come just 40 years later with the work of the Impressionists. Constable's later work becomes more and more impressionistic, although this could also be detected in some earlier work, especially in his handling of white and dashes of yellow and red. Now, however, the pure color and dazzling strokes are not just a part of the composition but make up the very essence of the scene.

For many years it was thought that this painting was a sketch for *The Valley Farm* (1835), of more or less the same time. However, it seems that Constable simply painted a scene that had residues from the past and that also included motifs which would turn up in other, later paintings.

A SUFFOLK CHILD: *SKETCH FOR*
THE VALLEY FARM (*C.* 1835)
Courtesy of the V & A Picture Library

*T*HIS child, also seen in the finished painting of *The Valley Farm* (1835), is a pretty little peasant girl. One supposes her age to be somewhere between eight and 12 years. She is almost certainly expected to work on the farm, which her parents probably tend in exchange for a tied cottage and a small weekly wage. Her parents are probably good, god-fearing people who have taught her to be industrious, good and Christian. Her golden hair is tied with a scarf. Her face is innocent and far-reaching, looking out to nature and perhaps to God. Her hands are gently clasped in her lap, her back is slightly bent forwards and her posture is hunched.

The sketch is beautifully drawn in pencil and watercolor and, despite the clichés, is a fine portrayal of a young peasant girl. The sketches for *The Valley Farm* (1835) include this young girl. Evidently, as Constable wrote to a friend between 1833 and 1835, he was "foolishly bent on" a large picture which was probably *The Valley Farm* and associated sketches.

This child appears sitting in a boat in the finished painting of 1835, which was exhibited at the Royal Academy and sold for £300 to the collector Robert Vernon.

AN ASH TREE (C. 1835)
Courtesy of the V & A Picture Library

THIS pencil drawing is a companion piece to a similar drawing that Constable made as a study for *The Valley Farm* (1835). Although the sketch of a tree may simply represent a tree, in Constable's idiom a specific tree may mean far more. Rather as a shepherd recognizes individual sheep in his flock, Constable held a

dialogue with nature that only an artist who observes and studies each individual aspect of the landscape could.

This tree may have been redrawn from an earlier study in order for Constable to illustrate his final lecture at the Royal Academy in 1836. In the lecture, Constable mentioned a tree upon which a sign had been nailed: "I made this drawing when she [the tree] was in full health and beauty; on passing some time afterwards, I saw, to my grief, that a wretched board had been nailed to her side, on which was written in large letters, "All vagrants and beggars will be dealt with according to law."' He continues to explain that the tree, evidently feeling the "disgrace", began to wither from its top branches, until eventually, "... this beautiful creature was cut down to a stump, just high enough to hold the board."

Note that nothing is mentioned about the fate of the poor woman who sits with her child beneath the tree.

An Oak in Dedham Meadows (1827)
Courtesy of the V & A Picture Library. (See p. 184)

248

SKETCH FOR THE VALLEY FARM (C. 1835)
Courtesy of the V & A Picture Library

*T*HIS is a compositional sketch for *The Valley Farm* that was exhibited at the Royal Academy in 1835. Willy Lott's house can be seen prominently, although shrouded by bushes and trees. The house, which can be seen in many of Constable's paintings, is notable in *The Haywain* (1821) and *The Mill Stream* (1814).

It has been said that Constable had something of an obsession with Willy Lott and his house, and the continued use of the house in his later work may represent a "desperate attempt to recreate the past." This is possible but it is equally reasonable to suppose that Constable worked away from Suffolk during the 1830s and that much of his work was carried out in his studio and not on location. He therefore made use of sketches and drawings he had made many years earlier, never tiring of the theme of Suffolk, especially Willy Lott's house.

Several pencil and oil sketches of this same composition exist. In the final painting, which is now at the Tate Gallery in London, the boat shifts further to the right of the composition and the young peasant girl is sitting down, being punted across the lake by a standing man.

The Haywain (c. 1821)
Courtesy of the V & A Picture Library. (See p. 138)

STONEHENGE (1835–37)
Courtesy of the V & A Picture Library

*T*HE atmosphere of Salisbury seems to be the essence of this study. This sketch for the watercolor of 1836 evokes the plains of Salisbury, Stonehenge and the intense loneliness of the place to great effect. The permanence of the stone against the transience of nature and man is made strikingly obvious. The sketch is made from a drawing in nature of 1820. It is remarkable that Constable could turn an eerie drawing into an intense watercolor that, some 15 years later, could evoke all the intensity vital to express the mood of a place.

The sky is imbued with all the sensibility that culminated in the unusually hostile sky of the finished watercolor. The crouched figure appears dwarfed by both stones and landscape, reminding us that Constable felt constantly in awe, not only of nature, but also of his duty to inspire the depth of this feeling in his painting.

A SLUICE, PERHAPS ON THE STOUR:
TREES IN THE BACKGROUND (C. 1830–36)
Courtesy of the V&A Picture Library

*T*HIS oil sketch on paper was probably painted in the last period of Constable's working life. It may be useful to consider that this sketch was drawn after the watercolor *View in the Grounds of Arundel Castle* (1835), and that the subsequent thoughts Constable had about the picturesque, both in painting and in nature, inform this sketch.

Here, it appears that Constable is using a similar "broken ruggedness" that he wished would influence his painting. The scene is dynamic, dramatically shifting as we look from left to right. The water rushes from the sluice, over which there is a footbridge, towards the foreground. The water, otherwise gray and lightless, has highlights of white foam created by the surf from the sluice.

In the foreground a dense mass of yellow-green foliage rises up to the left, hugging the stream. A tree, dark and blowing in a stormy wind, elevates towards a sky of slate gray, pink, and white. The sky is moving from left to right, turning the light into dark and the stillness into a symphony of rushing, crashing, and rustling. Two birds fly towards the tree above the insignificant figure in a red garment sitting on the bank.

***View in the Grounds of
Arundel Castle*** **(1835)**
*Courtesy of the V & A Picture
Library. (See p. 236)*

STONEHENGE (1836)
Courtesy of the V & A Picture Library

EXHIBITED by Constable at the Royal Academy in 1836, this watercolor was initially composed in pencil in 1820 on Constable's only known visit to Salisbury Plain. He accompanied the painting with the following inscription:

"The mysterious monument of Stonehenge, standing remote on a bare and boundless heath, as much unconnected with the events of past ages as it is with the uses of the present, carries you back beyond all historical records into the obscurity of a totally unknown period."

The effect of light in the composition is strange: sometimes the image can appear monochrome, possibly because of the medium and the fact that the color is both intense and translucent. The sky is violent. Nature is unforgiving and the stones will protect nothing and no one except their own secret. A figure, and its shadow and another figure walking mid-ground, are dwarfed by the stones.

Constable extended the picture. The hare in the lower left-hand corner running out of the picture is pasted on as a separate piece. The sky cascades on to the landscape, a compositional device that gives the illusion of light and also contrasts with, yet reflects the stone: heavy and light, hard and soft, permanent and transient.

AUTHOR BIOGRAPHIES AND ACKNOWLEDGMENTS

To my son Irwin, and little Rick.
And a million thanks to Sasha and Josephine at The Foundry.
Mandi Gomez studied art history at the University of Essex. She gained her Masters degree from the School of Oriental and African Studies in London, where she now works as a writer and editor.

Karen Hurrell is Canadian-born and educated, and is the author of several art books, including works on Monet, Renoir, Turner, and the Pre-Raphaelites. She also writes widely on health matters and lives in London with her two sons.

While every endeavor has been made to ensure the accuracy of the reproduction of the images in this book,we would be grateful to receive any comments or suggestions for inclusion in future reprints.

With thanks to AKG and the V&A Picture Library for assistance with sourcing the pictures for this series of books.With thanks to Josephine Cutts, Claire Dashwood, and Karen Villabona.

To my father, who told me to write stories in my head when I couldn't sleep. I never stopped. —ML

For Graham and Harrison, with all of my love —CC

Dial Books for Young Readers
An imprint of Penguin Random House LLC, New York

Text copyright © 2020 by Melanie LaBarge
Illustrations copyright © 2020 by Caroline Corrigan

Visit us online at penguinrandomhouse.com
Printed in China • ISBN 9780593108727
10 9 8 7 6 5 4 3 2 1

Design by Caroline Corrigan and Lily Malcom
Text set in Miller Text and ITC Franklin Gothic

The art for this book was created digitally.

Dial Books
for Young Readers

WOMEN ARTISTS A TO Z

by
Melanie LaBarge

illustrated by
Caroline Corrigan

MIRKA MORA

Mirka made paintings that look like lush forests afloat with colorful angels. Her mix of animals, winged cherubs, and humans swirl together in nature, filling her pieces with the magic of the world around us and inside of us.

A is for Angel

B is for Box

BETYE SAAR

Betye is known for assembling materials within a box. She filled the boxes with personal treasures and found objects in order to tell stories, celebrate Black history and culture, and to confront and examine racist stereotypes and images.

C is for Color

HELEN FRANKENTHALER

Helen created pieces called color field paintings—large as fields and full of color. Instead of painting on an easel, she tried something new: laying the canvas on the floor and soaking it in flowing paints that seeped into the fabric.

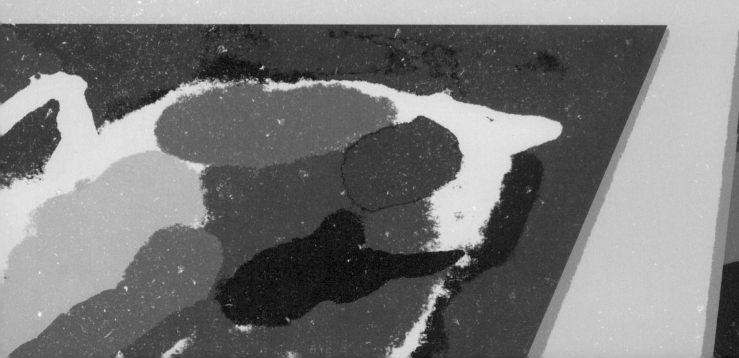

D is for Dots

YAYOI KUSAMA

Yayoi loves dots and for more than fifty years she has put dots on canvases, walls, trees, and her clothes and body! She has even created Infinity Rooms where people can enter and be completely surrounded by dots.

E is for Eggs

KAY SAGE

Kay was a surrealist painter, meaning she showed ordinary things in a way that is new or unfamiliar. She often put eggs in paintings of landscapes and buildings. Eggs in the hallway! A giant egg leaning on the stairs! That's surreal.

F is for Flower

GEORGIA O'KEEFFE

Georgia captivated the world with her flowers. She would paint the same flower over and over, bigger and bigger, closer and closer. Her art shows us how to look deeply at everything and to see nature in a whole new way.

G is for Grid

AGNES MARTIN

Agnes was inspired by a vision to make grid paintings. She used rulers to draw rectangles in pencil across the surface of her painted square canvases. Many of her grids were so big that she had to use a ladder to reach them.

H is for Horse

JAUNE QUICK-TO-SEE SMITH

Jaune's art confronts the mistreatment of Indigenous people and land in the United States. She often includes horses as both a personal symbol—her father was a horse trader—and a political one: reminding us of the ties between humans and nature.

I is for Ink

ELIZABETH CATLETT

Elizabeth created art in many forms, from screen prints, to sculptures, to linocuts that used ink. She often centered the experiences of women and children, sculpting and stamping images of African American imagination, activism, and love into art.

J is for Jolly

JUDITH LEYSTER

Judith was a painter more than three hundred years ago! Many thought her jolly paintings had been made by men, because working female artists were so rare at the time. It is easy to spot her work, though: She always painted a star into her signature.

K is for Kitchen

LEONORA CARRINGTON

Leonora's paintings of magical, mythical creatures began in the kitchen. She mixed eggs and pigment to make a paint called egg tempera. Just like a chef or a scientist, Leonora loved transforming ordinary ingredients into something magnificent.

CARMEN HERRERA

Carmen paints large blocks of color side by side onto canvases so that in the space where the two colors meet, lines come to life! She spent more than ten years painting a series with only white and green called *Blanco y Verde*.

L is
for
Line

M is for Marble

EDMONIA LEWIS

Edmonia sculpted mountains of marble into smooth, life-size human figures. While perfecting classic techniques of sculpture, she carved out the stories of Native Americans and newly freed Africans and West Indians.

N is for Nature

MAYA LIN

Maya uses natural materials—often recycled—such as glass, metal, wood, and dirt. Her work helps us think about our environment by resizing and reimagining parts of nature, such as when she constructed a whole field of rolling hills to mirror the ocean's waves!

O is for
Opposites

HILMA AF KLINT

Hilma was always trying to paint the unseen, from the tiniest parts of life, like the cells we are made up of, to the expansive energy of the universe. Many of her paintings contain the balance of opposites—light and dark, small and large, up and down.

MARIA MARTINEZ

Maria molded coils of clay into both beautifully delicate *and* strong pieces of pottery. The black-on-black design was part of her San Ildefonso Pueblo community's tradition in which shapes and mythical creatures appear in the shiny glaze painted on the darkened clay.

P is for Pottery

Q is for Quilt

GEE'S BEND

The Gee's Bend Collective doesn't refer to one artist but to many generations of African American women in Gee's Bend, Alabama. They gather to weave community *and* geometry into modern art quilts that grace clotheslines and museum walls.

R is for Roots

FRIDA KAHLO

Frida made paintings that were small in scale but very large in impact. She created colorful and revolutionary self-portraits filled with an imagery rooted in her Mexican identity and culture, and influenced by the Indigenous roots of Mexico.

S is for Spider

LOUISE BOURGEOIS

Louise's large metal spider sculptures are lovingly called *maman*—the French word for mother—in honor of her own maman, Josephine. Louise spent so many years of her life making spiders, both big and small, that she is often referred to as "Spider Woman."

T is for Technique

LOÏS MAILOU JONES

Loïs used a multitude of techniques to make art. She designed vibrant textiles, painted realistic portraits, watercolored cityscapes *and* landscapes, and collaged abstract paintings with African and Haitian imagery. As a teacher, she also encouraged generations of artists to try their own different approaches.

U is
for
Unique

ALICE NEEL

Alice painted friends, family, and neighbors, capturing each person's unique energy and style. Unlike many artists of her era who focused on abstract work, she chose to create portraits that allowed each individual's personality to come through with her one-of-a-kind style of painting.

V is for Veil

HELEN ZUGHAIB

Helen paints women wearing the abaya—a veiled garment
worn by some Muslim women—in much of her work. She
even reimagines famous pieces of Western art by including
Eastern imagery to create a dialogue between cultures that
moves beyond stereotypes.

W is for Wood

URSULA VON RYDINGSVARD

Ursula is a sculptor who has worked with cedar for many years.
The pungent smell of wood lingers long after she's done sculpting it.
Some of Ursula's imaginative pieces are small enough to hang on walls,
while others need a wide outdoor space.

X is for EXposure

DOROTHEA LANGE

Dorothea was a photographer known for her empathetic portraits. Her photos—or exposures—revealed the effects of poverty and inequality on families across the United States during the Great Depression.

Y is for Yarn

XENOBIA BAILEY

Xenobia's yarn-based art weaves together the traditions of African American, Indigenous, and Eastern cultures. Her mandalas are spiraling symbols of joy, art, resilience, and our connection to one another.

AUTHOR'S NOTES ON THE ARTISTS

MIRKA MORA
1928–2018 • Paris, France

Mirka and her family hid from Nazis in the forests of France when she was a teenager and the imagery of winged figures amongst trees can be seen throughout her entire career. As a young woman, she moved to Melbourne, Australia, and shook up the contemporary art world there. Her pieces ranged from small dolls to large murals and even a trolley car—and angels found their way into her artwork again and again!

What things do you see in nature that you would like to paint? Fill your art with something you love, over and over again!

BETYE SAAR
b. 1926 • Los Angeles, California

Betye's technique, called assemblage, utilizes objects that you can find in your own home. Some objects she used include dolls, photographs, drawings, mirrors, jewelry, fabric, feather, rocks, and letter blocks. Betye was part of the Black Arts Movement of the 1960s and 1970s, and she included historical figures such as Civil Rights activist Rosa Parks and blues singer Bessie Smith in her art. She often used boxes to examine the prejudicial ideas and imagery that grew out of racism, the institutionally supported mistreatment of people based on the color of their skin.

What would you put in your own assemblage box? What or whose story would it tell?

HELEN FRANKENTHALER
1928–2011 • New York, New York

Helen perfected her soak-stain technique by drenching the canvas in paints thinned with turpentine. She worked with her whole body, often dancing around her paintings or propping herself up on her arms while lying across the giant canvas! She claimed that by painting with movement she could feel the art flowing through her arms and spilling onto the canvas. Her paintings are referred to as abstract expressionism because they don't look realistic but they convey the feelings she had while painting them.

Name your favorite color! What image or feeling would you try to soak into a giant canvas?

YAYOI KUSAMA
b. 1929 • Nagano, Japan

Yayoi uses art to help her understand the vastness of the universe. She sees earth, and even each one of us, as one dot in an endless, infinite cosmos of dots. She has been making paintings, sculptures, performances, and installations using dots for over half a century. She also uses light and mirrors in her Infinity Rooms to create the feeling of infinite space, and each room has a unique name such as *Longing for Eternity* (2017) and *My Heart Is Dancing into the Universe* (2018). Since her childhood Yayoi has made art to cope with hallucinations and panic.

If you could cover anything in dots, what would it be? Make a pattern that you think expresses the vastness of the universe!

KAY SAGE
1898–1963 • Albany, New York

Kay moved all over the world, married a prince, left the prince, moved from Rome, Italy, to Paris, France, and back to New York again. In addition to eggs, her paintings quite often included stairs, columns, archways, curtains, and empty landscapes. Kay was a unique surrealist painter in that unlike many other surrealists she used a very neutral, limited number of colors in her pieces. Kay never explained why she chose to paint eggs, leaving their meaning up to our own imaginations!

Paint, draw, or color an egg in a place that you would never expect. What object would you choose to paint into a background to make it feel surreal?

GEORGIA O'KEEFFE
1887–1986 • Sun Prairie, Wisconsin

Georgia's work often contained the places she lived in and loved: from skyscrapers in New York City, to the mountains of Lake George, and the desert landscapes of her chosen home in Santa Fe, New Mexico. Georgia became famous for the way she painted flowers so close up, making them larger than life. Her art played with our sense of scale, meaning the size of the object (the flower) in relation to the size of something else (the size of the canvas or the size of the viewer). She did not like the way people claimed to know what her flowers meant or the way they called her a woman artist instead of simply "artist."

How would you paint a flower: up close or far away, a single stem or a whole field? What is your favorite flower?

AGNES MARTIN
1912–2004 • Macklin, Saskatchewan, Canada

Agnes often used 6-by-6-foot square canvases for her grids because they mimicked adult human size. Her initial inspiration for drawing grids included her thoughts about trees, which she transformed into a totally original vision. She even made a piece titled *The Tree* (1964). Agnes' art was special because she didn't cover up the imperfections of her own hand-drawn lines, whereas other artists wanted to make pieces without a trace of the person who made it! Agnes' work is minimal, meaning that her art is limited in color and consists of simple shapes or geometry rather than detailed images.

What shapes would you graph with your own pencils and rulers? Draw a tree in a brand-new way!

JAUNE QUICK-TO-SEE SMITH
b. 1940 • Flathead Indian Reservation, Montana
Jaune is an enrolled member of the Confederated Salish and Kootenai Nation in Montana. Though her painting, collage, and printmaking are referred to as abstract, her subject matter is often directly related to her Native American identity. In addition to horses, her work also often incorporates maps to bring awareness to the forcible removal and displacement of Indigenous peoples across the United States. Her collage work is an example of mixed media, meaning that it combines a mix of materials together on a single surface.

Which animal would you paint into the story of your life? What materials would you use to create a collage?

ELIZABETH CATLETT
1915–2012 • Washington, DC
Elizabeth was born in the United States but spent many years of her life living and creating art in Mexico. In both countries, she created graphic art by cutting out an image, covering it in ink or paint, and stamping it onto another surface—which allowed her to reproduce the same image over and over again. Elizabeth often made linocuts (cut linoleum), woodcuts (cut wood), and screen prints (all of which use ink!) to transfer her designs. She also sculpted wood, marble, and onyx. Her work included many famous African American subjects, such as Harriet Tubman and eighteenth-century poet Phyllis Wheatley.

Create an image that you would love to stamp over and over again! Which remarkable person's story would you like to include in your own art?

JUDITH LEYSTER
1609–1660 • Haarlem, Netherlands
Judith's paintings often included jolly folk: people smiling, dancing, playing instruments, and more. When she created her *Self-Portrait* (c.1630) it was very special because she looked comfortable (and confident!) as an artist during a time when men often didn't allow women to work, much less as painters. The name Leyster translates to *lodestar* or *lead star,* meaning a star that leads travelers.

It was the discovery of her star signature that led art historians to realize that works attributed to an artist named Frans Hals were actually done by Judith instead!

What would you paint to feel jolly? Create your very own artistic signature or symbol to sign your work!

LEONORA CARRINGTON
1917–2011 • Clayton Green, England
Leonora's paintings often contained elements of otherworldly beings, animals acting and dressing like humans, or allegorical stories from myths. She moved from England to Mexico and together with fellow surrealist painter and friend Remedios Varo, Leonora explored the relationship between women's traditional roles of having a family and working in the home—specifically the kitchen—with the act of making art. Leonora loved to play with food, making new and sometimes very strange creations for her friends and dinner guests.

What is the most magical food you have ever eaten? What is in your kitchen that you could you create art with?

CARMEN HERRERA
b. 1915 • Havana, Cuba
Carmen has spent most of her life living and working in New York City. She initially trained as an architect (like Maya Lin!), someone who designs and creates the plans for buildings. Carmen was 81 years old when she sold her first painting and 101 when she achieved her first retrospective—in which a large collection of her art was shown at a gallery. She creates her lines not by drawing them with a ruler (like Agnes Martin) but by painting colors side by side. At 104 she is still making her amazing line paintings!

What two colors would you put in a painting to make lines? What simple shape would you use to express a feeling?

EDMONIA LEWIS
1844–1907 • Greenbush, New York
Edmonia was born free to a Chippewa mother and a West Indian father and she gained international recognition as a sculptor at a time when slavery was still legal in the United States. She studied and worked in Rome, Italy, despite the fact that sculpting was seen as a man's art at the time. Society thought that women lacked the necessary strength—but this did not stop Edmonia. Her sculptures were referred to as neoclassical, or "new classical," in style and her main medium was Carrara marble. One of her sculptures—*Cleopatra*—required more than three thousand pounds of marble!

What would you carve out of marble? Find someone who *you* would want to see celebrated as a sculpture!

MAYA LIN
b. 1959 • Athens, Ohio

Maya studied architecture at Yale; she was chosen from thousands to design the Vietnam Veterans Memorial when she was only twenty-one! Much of Maya's work is installation, a type of art created with the experience of space in mind. It can move or stay in one location but maintains the same sense of placement and purpose. Maya's art often changes the landscape of the earth or brings the earth inside, so that we can see our relationship with nature in new ways. She works with natural elements to educate and expand awareness about the impact of human practices on the environment and the effects of climate change.

What landscape would you want to shape with your art? Try to make art out of objects you recycle at home!

HILMA AF KLINT
1862–1944 • Karlsburg Palace, Sweden

Hilma formally studied art for many years before experimenting with spiritual art endeavors, or séances. She and four other women (called *de Fem* or *The Five*) would hold séances to channel the life force of famous painters into the work they were creating. In this way she was one of the first abstract expressionist painters because her art was working to create a feeling or energy on the canvas rather than capture the likeness of something she was looking at.

If you could talk to any artist, past or present, who would it be? Paint two opposite things on each side of a piece of paper or canvas and find a way for them to meet in the middle!

MARIA MARTINEZ
1887–1980 • San Ildefonso Pueblo, New Mexico

Maria learned how to make pottery by watching other people in her Pueblo village. She spent years traveling and teaching others the traditional Pueblo coil technique of pottery: stacking thin, snake-like ribbons of clay, and molding them by hand (rather than using the pottery wheel). One image that often appeared in Maria's pottery was Avanyu, the guardian of water in Pueblo culture who is depicted as a swimming serpent flowing around her pieces.

What would you make with clay? Look around you to find an everyday object that has a design you love.

GEE'S BEND COLLECTIVE

The original Gee's Bend quilt makers are descendants of enslaved people brought to Boykin, Alabama. While the practices and patterns of African American quilting vary across the United States, the modern and abstract patterns made by Gee's Bend are truly one of a kind. Quilts are often not given the same recognition as painting or sculpture in the mainstream art community because they are a form of applied art, meaning art made from the transformation of everyday objects (just like Maria Martinez's pottery), but the Gee's Bend Collective has helped change the way we view quilts with their unique vision and story.

What kinds of fabric and designs would you include in your quilt? Who in your community would you like to make art with?

FRIDA KAHLO
1907–1954 • Coyoacan, Mexico City, Mexico

Frida is best known for her self-portraits, which blended the real and the fantastical. Frida suffered an injury as a young woman and began her most well-known portraits in earnest when a device was built to allow her to paint while recovering in bed. As she healed, she became the focus of her art (a mirror was attached to her bed!), but Frida always included specific elements, on and around herself, to tell a story with each self-portrait. Many of her works contain the imagery of roots, including two paintings of herself: *Roots* (1943) and *Self-Portrait Along the Border Line Between Mexico and the United States* (1932).

What would you want to include in your own self-portrait? To what or whom do you feel rooted? Draw your connection to the place or person in your own way!

LOUISE BOURGEOIS
1911–2010 • Paris, France

Louise worked throughout her almost one hundred years of life, making paintings, sculptures, tapestries, and drawings. Though Louise was French, she made a lot of her art in New York City. Louise's mother, or maman, the person who inspired her large spider sculptures, was a weaver and Louise's best friend. She saw her mother in the way spiders weaved their beautiful webs and protected their babies. Some of these maman sculptures are up to thirty feet tall!

What creature most reminds you of your best friend? How BIG or small would you make a sculpture of it and why?

LOÏS MAILOU JONES
1905–1998 • Boston, Massachusetts

Loïs was part of the Harlem Renaissance—a movement during the 1920s that started in Harlem, New York—when African American artists thrived, creating art, music, and literature that reshaped the whole world. One of her first careers was making textiles (fabrics that have patterns weaved into or placed directly upon them) that vibrated with color and imagery. Then she moved her focus from fabric to paint and began teaching these techniques to others, while still making art. Loïs taught fine arts for more than four decades at Howard University and one of her students was Elizabeth Catlett!

Draw a picture inspired by the most important teacher you've ever had. What art technique do you most want someone to teach you?

ALICE NEEL
1900–1984 • Gladwyne, Pennsylvania
Alice was a rebel—she defied her parents' wishes and put herself through art school, then moved to Greenwich Village in New York City. She worked for the Federal Arts Project, part of the Works Progress Administration, a federally funded program during the Great Depression when the government invested directly in employing artists. After moving to Spanish Harlem, Alice began to paint portraits full-time, for decades, within the comfort of her apartment. Her painting *Andy Warhol* (1970) showed the famous pop artist in a light that was very different from how the world had seen him before or after.

Who would you paint from your neighborhood? List three things that are unique about yourself and try to put them in your art!

HELEN ZUGHAIB
b. 1959 • Beirut, Lebanon
Helen and her family were forced to leave Lebanon in 1975 due to civil war, and she now lives in Washington, DC. Her work has been purchased and given as gifts by many politicians—including President Barack Obama! Helen mixes iconic paintings with the image of veiled women; two of the artists whose works she reimagined (shown on pages 48 and 49) are Piet Mondrian (center canvas) and Pablo Picasso (right canvas). Her work confronts stereotypes—or prejudiced ideas and beliefs about certain groups—with a spectrum of joyful imagery.

What would you wear to have your portrait painted? If you could re-create a famous painting, which would you choose?

URSULA VON RYDINGSVARD
b. 1942 • Deensen, Lower Saxony, Germany
Ursula spent much of her childhood surviving World War II and being relocated from one Polish refugee camp to another. After moving to the United States she studied art and began working as a sculptor. From small sculptures, to pieces large as towers, Ursula finds a way to mold hard materials (like wood, bronze, copper or steel) in ways that make them gentle, curved, malleable and entirely new. She sculpts in many mediums but has focused mainly on wood from cedar trees, the lovely smell of which enhances the sensory experience of the art.

What shape would you turn a piece of wood into? If your art could have a smell, which smell would you choose and why?

DOROTHEA LANGE
1895–1965 • Hoboken, New Jersey
Dorothea studied photography at Columbia University. In San Francisco, she started taking pictures of people waiting in line for food or aid during the Great Depression. After seeing those images, the Resettlement Administration gave her a job documenting the effects of poverty and economic insecurity across the country. Her most famous exposure is *Migrant Mother* (1936) taken of Florence Owens Thompson and her children. Dorothea's pictures have exposed issues even after her death. Her images from Japanese internment camps taken in 1942 were only recently made public; they brought to light the unseen experiences and traumas that Japanese Americans survived in the United States.

Take a picture! Then look to see what the image reveals that you didn't notice before. What do you think needs to be photographed for the world to see?

XENOBIA BAILEY
b. 1955 • Seattle, Washington
Xenobia was born with the name Sherilyn but found that Xenobia, the name of an ancient African warrior woman, suited her better. Her backgrounds in design, ethnomusicology, and needlework all influence her art. Xenobia is often referred to as a fiber artist and her crochet and knitting is inspired by a funk aesthetic, which centers around African American creativity, craft, poetry, and music. She's made hats, costumes, wall-sized pieces, and even whole tents from yarn! Xenobia also makes mandalas, a symbol often used by Buddhists and Hindus to show the totality of the universe and the connectivity of many into one.

Have you ever knit or crocheted something with yarn? What would you make your mandala out of and what colors would it be?

MARIA SIBYLLA MERIAN
1647–1717 • Free Imperial City of Frankfurt in the Holy Roman Empire (present-day Germany)
Maria's fascination with painting the natural world began when she started collecting and raising silkworms as a young girl! She learned all about metamorphosis—the process by which a caterpillar changes into a butterfly—through careful observation. While many artists painted insects, animals, or plants separate from each other, Maria painted them together. In fact, because she made art from what she witnessed over time, she changed science forever: She drew the full life cycle of insects when people still believed bugs came out of the dirt instead of hatching from eggs. She traveled to Suriname later in life to draw reptiles, snakes, and even caiman crocodiles!

Which animal would you most like to watch and draw? Draw some of your favorite animals together in one place.